Marlboro

W9-ARJ-284

My Fellow Americans

Other books by Malcolm Boyd

ARE YOU RUNNING WITH ME, JESUS?

FREE TO LIVE, FREE TO DIE

MALCOLM BOYD'S BOOK OF DAYS

THE FANTASY WORLDS OF PETER STONE
AND OTHER FABLES

AS I LIVE AND BREATHE:
STAGES OF AN AUTOBIOGRAPHY

EDITOR: THE UNDERGROUND CHURCH

My Fellow Americans

Malcolm Boyd

Holt, Rinehart and Winston

New York   Chicago   San Francisco

Wingate College Library

Copyright © 1970 by Malcolm Boyd

All rights reserved, including the right to reproduce
this book or portions thereof in any form.

Published simultaneously in Canada by Holt, Rinehart
and Winston of Canada, Limited.

Library of Congress Catalog Card Number: 78-118090

Sept. 23, 1975

First Edition

Designer: Bob Antler

SBN 03-085051-7

Printed in the United States of America

Grateful acknowledgment is made for excerpts from the following
sources:

Reprinted from *Young Man Luther, A Study in Psychoanalysis and
History*, by Erik H. Erikson. By permission of W. W. Norton & Company, Inc. Copyright © 1958, 1962 by Erik H. Erikson.

Reprinted from *The Wretched of the Earth*, by Frantz Fanon. By permission of Grove Press, Inc. Copyright © 1963 by *Presence Africaine*.

Excerpted from *Bread and Wine* by Ignazio Silone, a new version
translated from the Italian by Harvey Fergusson II. Copyright 1937
by Harper & Brothers. Copyright © 1962 by Atheneum House, Inc.
Reprinted by permission of Atheneum Publishers.

Reprinted from *All Quiet on the Western Front*, by E. M. Remarque by
permission of Little, Brown and Company.

065116

051516

Introduction

When I was a child, I heard Franklin Delano Roosevelt open his famous fireside chats—those informal presidential talks to the nation over the radio—with the greeting, "My fellow Americans." Of course, he was a highly controversial figure, but for me these words were always suggestive of limitless possibilities, conjuring up in my mind a picture of vastly different people held together only by their kinship in that curious cultural amalgamation, "Americans." It was a mystery to me then, how Roosevelt could make so many people feel they were at a gigantic town meeting, and that their own hopes and concerns were being powerfully articulated. Finally I realized that Roosevelt had a key resource, just as important as his charismatic personality and superb voice: his wife constantly traveled around the country and reported back to him on what she heard, and her vocation was listening.

Now is a time when listening is especially needed, but also

one when it may have become more difficult for many of us. But the truth is: to listen is never easy. I recall an afternoon many years ago when, as a campus chaplain, I was seated at my desk in the Episcopal student center at Colorado State University. A woman student, directly across from me, was trying to explain some pressing campus problem. Suddenly, even at the risk of being rude, I had to interrupt her.

"I'm sorry," I said. "I appear to be listening to you, but I'm not. I've been in counseling situations with different people all day, and I'm tired out. If what you have to say won't wait until tomorrow morning, let's take a half-hour break and I'll go for a short walk in the fresh air to clear my head. If it will wait, I'll see you at seven-thirty in the morning if you like."

The next day, when we resumed our conversation, both of us knew I was hearing what she said.

In the last few years, particularly since the publication of *Are You Running With Me, Jesus?*, I have been made into a minor celebrity of sorts, with my ideas frequently enlarged (and distorted) in headlines and prepackaged feature stories. Nevertheless, I cannot complain unduly about this, since I was free to use (as well as be used by) the media, and the truth is that most of my books, including the prayers and meditations, grew out of my own evolving lifestyle, my own ambiguities and questions. But when I finally, painfully, completed *As I Live and Breathe*, a partial autobiography, I was more determined than ever to look outside myself and my particular experience. Perhaps I had grown tired of hearing my own opinions, but I knew that what I really wanted was to find out more about other people's lives in America.

But whose lives? I was not trying to construct a sociological sample or an ethnically balanced political ticket; I was hoping to learn from people capable of illuminating major tension areas and unspoken dreams. At the outset, I rather thought it would be necessary to restrict my inquiries to celebrated names: a legendary writer, a distinguished spokesman for the peace movement, a prominent black leader, a contro- versial magazine editor, a prestigious political figure, and even a noted film star. Even then, however, I was planning no routine interviews; the idea was to live with my subjects for a week or more, after finding out as much about them and their backgrounds as possible; they would have to be willing to be available to talk in offguard as well as scheduled moments. Since the man's style, along with the kind of air breathed in his habitat, would be more important than the abstract ideas ex- pressed, it would be necessary to spend considerable time with those people whose lives intimately touched his.

Somehow—I am almost tempted to say, providentially— the book assumed its own form. It turned out that there was only one genuine celebrity in the collection—Hugh Hefner, whose calculated manufacture of layer upon layer of imagery had made him almost a public myth. In the course of my en- counter with Mr. Hefner, however, it was clear that I was in- volved with a human being as well as a communications and entertainment empire, a man who was both a mirror image and a challenge to an earlier myth of American innocence.

Next, I found myself looking into a broader picture of America, North and South combined, in which the heirs of Indian and Spanish intermarriage outnumbered the white "Anglos." This was the world opened up to me by a dynamic community of Chicanos (as Mexican-Americans, our second largest minority, prefer to be called), where I met one of the strongest personalities I have ever encountered, Rodolfo "Corky" Gonzalez. Gonzalez, founder of the Crusade for Jus- tice in Denver, a key center for Chicano political and cultural renewal in the Southwest, has a compelling dream of freedom and justice; a poet, he is entirely pragmatic in encouraging the development of independent leadership that can help translate this dream into reality.

After studying such powerful images of affluence and poverty, I was ready for other questions. There were nuances and surprises in both the success-story career and the life of personal sacrifice; what other examples could I find that would speak to today's nerve centers, helping us look more clearly at unexamined assumptions? In the last two interviews of the book I encountered men and women who were deeply in earnest about the possibility that our most primary western institution, the family, was no longer viable, and I spoke to a group of Vietnam war veterans whose agonized reflections on their experience undercut all the convenient clichés of both doves and hawks.

First it was the commune story, in which seven students, three men and four women, were free enough to allow me to discover the precarious early stage of a revealing experiment. Talking with them helped me to understand better what lies behind the demand for women's liberation, and their experience is also linked to questions increasingly raised as to what to do about sex, in relation to coupling versus individual identities. In the last resort, the commune members saw their efforts as a political action of grave importance, since they were asking for nothing less than the ultimate restructuring of the family in a capitalist society.

Finally, upsetting more of my preconceptions, I spent hours talking to the Vietnam veterans; despite the anguish of their recollections, what was perhaps most striking was the gratitude they expressed at having a chance to review their experience, and by searching for its essential truth, help others to understand it. Fortunately, as their accounts will make clear, they spoke as individuals, not as ideologues, and they have much to teach us about what we should expect when several hundred thousand of their comrades return to our rich and restless land. What had they learned about themselves, I asked them, about their fellow G.I.'s, the people called the Vietnamese, and what it means to be a soldier today? They were deeply concerned with the contrast between life in a poor, war-torn Asian country and our continent-wide shopping center, but they were even more confused as to whether they had come home as heroes or antiheroes.

Such deep contradictions, and others implicit in this book, can be reconciled only by Americans who learn to listen. Those who read quickly may at first believe that *My Fellow Americans* is less personal than my earlier work, but if they are attentive they will find that it is as autobiographical as any other I have written. It is true that the many different voices speaking directly here are not mine; they express sharply divergent views of what it means to be an American, or indeed a human being living in the 1970's, and I offer no alternative or "solution." It is even likely that some of the voices heard will provoke angry reactions, as if they have no right to say what they say, or express themselves in their own idiom. But I believe that all of us have been too prone to speak—and even to proclaim an answer to a question that was not asked—yet not sufficiently willing to give others an attentive hearing.

In this book, I have tried to listen.

MALCOLM BOYD

Los Angeles
February, 1970

My Fellow Americans

Wingate College Library

1

Hugh Hefner and *Playboy*

In the evaluation of the dominant moods of any historical period it is important to hold fast to the fact that there are always islands of self-sufficient order—on farms and in castles, in homes, studies, and cloisters—where sensible people manage to live relatively lusty and decent lives: as moral as they must be, as free as they may be, and as masterly as they can be. If we only knew it, this elusive arrangement *is* happiness. But men, especially in periods of change, are swayed by alternating world moods which seem to be artificially created by the monopolists and manipulators of an era's opinions, and yet could not exist without the highly exploitable mood cycles inherent in man's psychological structure. The two most basic alternating moods are those of carnival and atonement: the first gives license and leeway to sensual enjoyment, to relief and release at all cost; the second surrenders to the negative conscience which constricts, depresses, and enjoins man for what he has left unsolved, uncared for, unatoned. Especially in a seemingly rational and informed period like our own, it is obvious how blithely such moods overshadow universally available sets of information, finding support for luxurious thoughtlessness at one time, for panicky self-criticism at another. Thus we may say that beside and beyond a period's verifiable facts and official doctrines, the world image "breathes." It tends to expand and to contract in its perspectives, and to gain or lose solidity and coherence. In each careless period latent panic only waits for catastrophe—famines, pests and depressions, overpopulation and migration, sudden shifts in technology or in leadership—to cause a shrinkage in the world image, a kind of chill attacking the sense of identity of large masses.

It was a rainy day in New Haven; it had been a good year for me at Yale, but now I was anxious to get started on a new project, to get away from ivy-covered walls and see a bit of the country. Outside, on Elm Street, a downpour of water battered town and gown alike. Inside the dining room of Calhoun College, I was eating lunch with a Yale senior and his girl from Vassar. They asked me about my new book, and I told them that I would soon be going out to Chicago to work on it, and to interview Hugh Hefner.

"God, I detest him," the Vassar girl said.

"I don't see how you can spend any time with him or let him have any space in your book"—this from the Yale man, with a baleful look over his cup of black coffee.

"*Playboy*'s whole attitude toward women is disgusting," the girl went on, getting angrier. "Hefner must be *against* women. I loathe him."

"Jesus, he's so materialistic," the Yale man explained. "*Playboy* glorifies everything that's lousiest about America. Those hairless, frozen blondes—made up to look like the girl next door, and photographed in a phony, out-of-focus way. And those goddamn conformist ads. Everybody is sort of supernigger, with his unbelievable chick, his goddamn expensive car, his shitty correct suit and shaving lotion and pad. Christ. You shouldn't do it."

Three weeks later, I arrived at Chicago's O'Hare Airport.

Erik H. Erikson, *Young Man Luther* (New York, W. W. Norton & Co., the Norton Library Edition, 1962), p. 75.

Hefner's chauffeur, a genial Irishman, stood waiting at the gate. In a few minutes he had picked up my bags and carried them over to a sleek black limousine parked outside; we were ready for the ride to Hefner's house, which everyone referred to as The Mansion.

I settled back for the drive, noting appreciatively that the *Wall Street Journal*, the *Tribune*, and the *Sun-Times* were all stacked neatly at my feet. The chauffeur asked me if I would like a Pepsi-Cola. Thirsty for scalding hot coffee, I said that I would. He proceeded to open an iced bottle and pour it into a large paper cup. *This* knob in the back seat, he explained, would turn up the air conditioner. *That* knob dialed radio stations. *And* this button—the one directly to my left—made a kind of psychedelic screen light up at night. "You don't need to take drugs," he laughed, "in order to have a trip."

We reached downtown Chicago, passed the Ambassador-East, and turned into a driveway a half-block away. There was The Mansion. "Mr. Hefner isn't here, you know," the chauffeur told me; I allowed as how I did. "He's expected back from San Juan at ten-twenty tonight. He should be back here by eleven."

We entered the front door, then stood directly before a television camera. The chauffeur pushed a buzzer. Upon recognition by unknown powers within, a second door was opened for us. It seemed that a drawbridge had been lowered and we were crossing a moat.

"*Always* stand square in front of that camera," the chauffeur cautioned me. "Until they get to know you inside, it may take a few seconds for you to identify yourself."

In the hallway there was an abstract sculpture of a woman, but we moved quickly up red-carpeted stairs into another hallway, and finally entered the main room. As Hefner himself would later tell me, it was "truly baronial. You can practically walk into that fireplace. But somehow it's all done in good humor, just for the fun of it. We could have rented Boris Karloff to walk through on weekends."

A Picasso hung over the fireplace, and there was also a

de Kooning and a Pollock. Two medieval figures in armor stood across the room facing the fireplace. On one wall was an abstract painting of a sailor urinating in an outdoor commode, only his head and feet showing.

"At first people didn't understand the house wasn't a typical house," Hefner explained later. "The rhythm of the house is the rhythm of the people living inside it, not of the sun and the moon and the world outside. It's a world unto itself and within itself. You see, man is the only creature who can control his environment. Other men are already doing the same thing I am in different ways, and more will in the future. I control the clock with a twenty-four hour staff. Audiovisual equipment collects data for me to review later. Nothing says the day has to have twelve, sixteen, or twenty-four hours, or begin at seven A.M., three P.M., or midnight. The hours can function as an extension of a man instead of committing him to do certain things at certain times. For example, most men work in the daytime." In contrast, Hefner, on a typical day, goes to sleep at seven or eight A.M. and gets up at three in the afternoon. Meals served in The Mansion also ignore the traditional associations of particular foods at a particular time of day: there is a single menu, and one may order a filet mignon at six A.M. or scrambled eggs at three P.M. At request, too, one may view on a TV set the tape of a Barbra Streisand special produced two years before, or go swimming at midnight, seven A.M., noon, or seven P.M.

One of the butlers introduced himself; he belonged to the second shift of the three complete staffs of servants working inside around the clock The Mansion. When he had carried my bags to the guest apartment I would occupy, it turned out that it was situated between two dormitories of Playboy "bunnies." Naturally, I was curious as to what these pretty girls were really like; their costume of bunny ears and bushy tails had made them seem strangely unreal to me. It turned out that those who worked at the Chicago Playboy Club could live at The Mansion for fifty dollars a month, not including meals.

As one should have expected, the girls were as different as a similar number of airline stewardesses, models, or secretaries. Indeed, it turned out that some of them had had difficulty in deciding whether to become a bunny or take one of these other jobs. There were white bunnies, black bunnies, big-city bunnies, and farm-girl bunnies—all mingled easily with the guests, especially in the dining room. (During my stay there, guests included Bishop John A. T. Robinson, the author of *Honest to God*, Buddy Rich, the musician, The Reverend Jesse Jackson of Chicago's "Operation Breadbasket," and Dr. Harvey Cox, the Harvard theologian and author of *The Secular City*.)

One girl, freckle-faced and sweet-looking, had recently had the distinction of appearing in the celebrated centerfold of *Playboy*, stripped to the buff; she reminded me of a Pi Phi or Kappa at a Midwestern college and could easily have played Jeanne Crain's daughter in a movie. Another, who wore the falsest eyebrows in memory, brushed back her long blonde hair and purred, "Do you like sex?" She was known for spicing her conversation with four-letter words and enjoyed telling stories about middle-aged Playboy Club customers, pathetically searching for Babbitt-like erotic adventure. Still another girl, a coed at a first-rate college, was simply working at the club for the summer. "Why don't the other girls get *up* in the morning and do something with themselves?" she asked me at nine A.M. as we swam together in the pool. "I mean, they don't seem to read or *any*thing." One bunny mysteriously suggested that she was really the mistress of a well-known movie star. Most of the girls were outwardly rather demure, but I also had a strange conversation with an extremely tense, pentup girl, terribly concerned about religion, and explaining to me over a grilled-cheese sandwich what she had learned in her study of the occult.

Waiting that first night for Hefner to arrive, one had the strange sense that he was already there, that even though he was away on a trip, the house continued to be inhabited by him. It was like what I felt when visiting William Randolph Hearst's California estate, San Simeon: the master was not dead, despite aging newspaper accounts to the contrary; at this very moment, he was working over papers at his desk up in the tower; soon he would be seated, laughing, at the majestic dining-room table (which, at his insistence, bore an undisguised ketchup bottle) in the splendid hall with proud flags; later, one would be able to hear him speaking with Marion Davies as they strolled in the garden.

In the three weeks I stayed at The Mansion, there would be so many divergent opinions expressed about its master, but more significant than any single view was the growing awareness that even many of those living at the house or working with Hefner on one or another of his many projects found it hard to distinguish between the sense of his overall presence and the man himself. A member of the *Playboy* editorial staff, caught in the turmoil of big-magazine politics, would pour out his frustration about the editor who lived only a few blocks away from the editorial offices and never visited them. Hefner's wing of The Mansion was an unassailable fortress within a walled city; this helped to account for the feeling, while watching a *Playboy* staff member, after several months on the magazine, finally meet the boss—briefly, and over a handshake—one night in the main room, that one was watching a small, frightened boy make the acquaintance of a sophisticated, gregarious, and pipe-smoking bishop.

Love-hate feelings about Hefner quickly emerged from both old and new associates on *Playboy*. "His inner core? We don't know what's in it," an executive confessed. "A beautiful light or a can of worms—I've often wondered." Another editor, while discussing Hefner with me, reached across his desk to a bookshelf and took down an anthology of American poetry. He checked the index for Edwin Arlington Robinson, found the page he wanted, and said solemnly, "Maybe Hugh's another Richard Cory"—and proceeded to read me the whole poem, slowly and with emphasis.

The Playboy building itself was one of Chicago's sky-scrapers, the former Palmolive Building, but everyone in it seemed to revolve psychologically in a constant orbit around proliferating images of the absent boss who, during most of their work day, was sleeping gently in his celebrated circular bed only a short distance away. Hefner himself told me that he had only been in the building a handful of times. "The first time was in the middle of the night when it was raining. I was out walking. We'd laid out millions and I hadn't yet wandered over, even though it's only a few blocks from The Mansion. It turned out the guard didn't know who I was—but he finally let me in. And I went back for the open house that was the official opening of the building."

Visiting the Playboy Building, one felt great waves of feeling—envy, hostility, love, and anguish—constantly wash-ing against The Mansion. "It's a damned mausoleum," an im-portant magazine aide complained. "That huge English mead hall. Those gigantic works of art and coats of armor. And most of the people there are corpses and zombies. Oh, I know there are some who are really great, enjoyable, stimulating, but in that atmosphere they encapsulate themselves in a shell of shiny armor. You can't get to them; they're a slick sophisti-cated shell. Nobody quite touches."

Why did these men in Hefner's own organization speak so critically of him? Partly out of frustration, I thought. *They* worked hard for the magazine too, yet had not made millions of dollars or achieved world fame. Also they were obviously smarting under hurt. The Master paid them well and gave them editorial freedom, but he had left them behind, or at least outside his private life. They could observe it inside The Mansion, from time to time, when they were invited to a large party or a movie screening, but his life was clearly his own business. It lay well beyond the pale of their superficial involve-ment in it. They compulsively had to show an outsider such as myself that they did not *care*. In this gesture, of course, they revealed the aching care they suffered. All these pent-up feelings of theirs came through to me between the lines of what they said.

A less alienated view is available from an executive suite that occupied the corner looking up Michigan Avenue in the direction of The Mansion, where I chatted with A. C. Spectorsky, editorial director and associate publisher of *Playboy* since May 1, 1956. Author of *The Exurbanites* and an exciting figure in the New York publishing scene, Spectorsky gave up the East to work for Hefner and start a new life in Chicago.

"My first secretary when I came here was the most popular magazine Playmate up to that time," he reminisced. "We shared a tiny office about the size of this desk. Hef discovered I was a faithful husband. 'I finally found out what gives with you and your wife.' he said one day. 'You're both so sophisticated you practice fidelity for kicks.' "

The interview with Spectorsky took place one busy Friday afternoon, and developed into a near three-hour conversation, at the end of which most secretaries had departed and a weekend calm had descended on the office. "To me, Hef is unique, a brilliant walking paradox," Spectorsky said. "He's always been a man of utter extremes. He can be bone-hard selfish, egocentric, anally retentive, suspicious, almost paranoid; he can also pour out love, humanity, act out all the beautiful clichés that cynics no longer believe possible. But he's not a bleeding heart. When he goes out on a limb, he's perfectly aware of the dangers to himself; he just does it as a matter of principle, without hesitation.

"Another paradox: his genuine intellect, and yet the degree to which his responses are mostly visceral. He's sometimes agonizingly patient with people he has little regard for, and brutally impatient with those he cares for. I've heard him say, 'You can finish that sentence if you want to, but I know the end of it, so let's get on.'

"Of course, I have an intensely personal feeling about him. It's been the most significant relationship in my adult life. And for damned near fourteen years. Still, we don't see each other a lot."

Spectorsky himself is immensely likable. There is an aristocratic elegance about him that exists alongside an earthy pragmatism. When an editorial deadline strikes, he can probably be mercilessly demanding, all the while retaining what would then seem an exasperating vestige of charm. Offered a fortune to write *the* book about Hefner and *Playboy*, he quickly declined; he has other literary projects in mind.

By now Spectorsky had warmed to his subject. In his shirt sleeves, he got up from behind his desk and began to move around the room. "Hefner is a profound practical psychologist," he went on. "At the same time, he can be completely fooled by people who are transparently obvious to everybody else."

There was a long pause, and the words were so muted as to be hardly audible: "There have been times when I've hated Hef more deeply than anybody I don't love. To hate him as much as I've hated him, you really have to love him."

Spectorsky looked out the window and sat down again. "Another paradox: he is a living process. He's got a growing edge that is raw and palpitating and susceptible. Almost like a blank infant brain that's going to be influenced by anything that impinges on it. Yet he's got a fixation on the past. Deep down, he's got a teenager's romantic attitude toward girls.

"Here's a man who believes he has no habits. 'I've created a totally controlled environment,' he says. But the fact is that he has established a fairly rigid pattern of conforming to his nonconformity." (Hefner later said: "Patterns are things I have control over. Yes, I'm a person of patterns and habits; besides, there is a great tendency toward this in the middle years. But what's remarkable is that I've broken from rigid patterns.")

"At first, it meant a great deal to Hef to be able to sleep while others went to work," Spectorsky went on. "So he evolved a metabolic rhythm that's just as rigid except it's one hundred eighty degrees out of phase. He resents sleeping. He feels it's a dreadful waste of time. There was something in the papers about the Russians inventing a machine to enable only one hour of sleep at night. 'I want one of those,' Hef said.

"He has profound insight into himself right up to that central core. It's like the nucleus of an atom. He believes his mind is an open book, but there are aspects of himself that are totally invisible to him. Of course, he'd deny it. He believes he knows himself through and through, but there's that opaque nimbus that's impenetrable."

Spectorsky took an important phone call, handled it quickly, lit a cigarette, and leaned back in his chair across the desk from me.

"Hef's creating a myth as he goes along," he said. "He keeps a scrapbook to externalize his identity. It's a great way to shoehorn history in the form you want it to take, but he can't delegate his myth to other people. Of course, it's a great scene for me; I can have the courage of Hef's convictions."

What about the magazine?

"It's at a period of peril. Not because of itself, but because of its success. You can become a dinosaur instead of a growing thing. A part of that danger is that our highly intuitive boss is growing older. When you have spearheaded a sexual revolution, what are you going to do for an encore?"

I asked Spectorsky what he thought of The Mansion.

"It serves a marvelous purpose. It's like a blank screen onto which our critics project their fantasies of what they would do if they had the money and freedom. 'What do they *do* in there?' They're just spieling off."

His opinion of Hefner's syndicated TV show, "Playboy After Dark," was far more negative:

"The TV show is embarrassing, precisely because it is more revealing than Hef realizes. Of course, it's sophomoric, but that's not the point. The point is, it's just an aspect of Hef, and not the whole man. I've seen nothing on that show to deduce that one was in the video presence of a tremendous intellect. It's unworthy of Hef; he's got a Harold Teen attitude to show business, and he's much too bright for that."

How did Spectorsky look at his own role as Hefner's editorial director and associate publisher of *Playboy?*

"I have my own private inviolate department—as a person, not speaking of the magazine—that I find myself betraying more than I would like. Not that I do so cynically. I've too much of a stake in being what I am to become what I might admire more. But isn't it better to be persuasive with seventeen million readers than to talk to yourself by editing *The Nation* or *The New Republic?* Between dissent and the establishment, *Playboy* has an important mediating role. And one of the great things about our editorial staff is that they *care* so profoundly."

I mentioned the familiar complaint that the staff didn't see much of Hefner.

"Yes," Spectorsky conceded, "he doesn't have much direct contact with them. But he does have great influence on them. It's just that he doesn't often want to be stimulated intellectually or moved spiritually or impinged upon. He likes to be with his close buddies; they're not stupid, but they are anti-intellectual. It's his way of tuning out. His recreation consists mostly of being distracted from thinking. He'll play games—risk or gin." (Later Hefner confirmed this: "I do relish certain contacts with intellectually stimulating people. But not within the staff. It's more contact with outside people that I like.")

It was obvious that Spectorsky felt that Hefner was a unique publisher. "He's Harold Ross with balls," he exclaimed. "The reason Ross made the *New Yorker* successful was that he was a provincial to whom the city was exciting."

"What's he going to do for an encore? What can he do in order to survive?"

Spectorsky considered the problem.

"Well, you've got to remember: Hef is in love with love. That's why it's hard for him to be in love with people. But recently he's learned the limitations of money. It was a great shock for him that all the money in the world couldn't produce the airplane he wanted. He was putting five and a half million into a plane, but he couldn't have it on order—he had to wait eighteen months. He told me, 'You should be able to buy time as well as things.' But he can't."

Spectorsky obviously cared about Hefner's future. Not in financial terms, since the man was worth over one hundred million dollars, but in ordinary human terms—thinking about a friend who was forty-three, and going through a key period of personal transition.

"There will come a point in his life," Spectorsky said softly, "when he suddenly realizes that there's more time behind him than ahead. What do you do when you're fifty and suddenly realize that twenty years later you're going to be seventy. The best part of you, as far as actuarial statistics go, is behind you.

"Certainly what's ahead for the magazine is going to be harder than what's behind. The pioneering part could be over if we let it be. Once, you *had* to be pioneering; now you feel you *should*. Of course, the day of our greatest peril is when we don't have any enemies. Our enemies are important to us."

It was time for us to leave, but Spectorsky wasn't quite finished; he didn't want to end with thoughts of old age or feelings of depression. "You see, he's not only a romanticist, but a fixated romanticist. He wants the romance of a teenager —and he has it. It's hard to believe, but Hef is completely unjaded.

"For example, I can remember a meeting we had about ten years ago, and Hef suddenly said, 'I'm dying to get into movies. I want to make foreign films.' Some would-be wiseguy remarked, 'The trouble with foreign films is that you have to go overseas.' And Hef just said, 'Well, then we'll start our own country.' "

It was past eleven on the first night of my visit to The Mansion, and I was seated in the main room, nursing a scotch and soda. I began to think wistfully of other nights at this same hour when, having just seen the TV news, I proposed to pick up a good book, when Hefner finally arrived, coming in from his own quarters. He bounded through the door cutting through the space that separated us. He was wearing pajamas and a bathrobe, which was to become almost a uniform for our interview sessions, and was clearly ready to go to work. We moved into the conference room inside his private quarters, where we were to hold our almost nightly talks, usually from around eleven P.M. to one or two A.M.

It was not the first time that I had seen Hefner. We had met before on different occasions and once, on two successive nights, had sat up very late together while we talked about diverse subjects and drank. So I commenced our conversation in a low-key mood, fearing the task I had set up for myself far more than the man who sat across from me. I did not really fear *him*, but only the possible impasses or misunderstandings that might lay ahead of us, as I attempted to paint his portrait— that is, to place him in the perspective that I saw and, indeed, to see the warts as well as the well-known smile.

I watched Hefner closely while he fixed himself Jim Beam and Coke, but there were no obvious clues. Here was a hand- some, athletic man who was moving into his forties, his emo- tions extraordinarily well-wrapped, a mythical success symbol, yet almost as much of an enigma to the public as Howard Hughes. He was just under six feet tall, weighed 180 pounds, had sharp brown eyes that looked straight at you. As he smiled and lit his pipe, he seemed open and at ease, but there was a wiry, aloof restlessness about him.

Since even before coming to Chicago I had felt that Hefner's image had overwhelmed the real person, I asked what he thought was his larger significance; had he become a symbol?

"For most people, first and foremost I represent that it's still possible to make it," he said. "I'm a self-made millionaire. I didn't get any help from any outside source. So—capitalism works. And I did it on creative ideas, not by stock manipula- tion, taking advantage of tax allowances, that kind of thing. I've showed that it's possible to be a liberal and anti-establish- ment and still be very successful. And those that find out are intrigued that I'm using a lot of my money to further icono- clastic ideas.

"I'm one of a handful of people who most represent the

sexual revolution. Not that I invented sex, of course, but I've done more than almost anyone to promote the idea of sexual freedom. Dr. William Masters says *Playboy* is the single most important source of sexual information in our society."

I asked Hefner about the highly publicized incident during the 1968 Democratic National Convention, when he was attacked by a policeman on a Chicago street. Had this experience radicalized him?

"The radicalism was already there," he replied. "But because of my reputation as someone private, living almost a cloistered existence in a mansion, the papers played up the fact of my suddenly taking a walk at night and running into trouble. Max Lerner and Jules Feiffer were houseguests that week, and the three of us, along with an executive on the magazine and one of my secretaries, decided to walk down to Lincoln Park and over to Old Town. There were just a few police around, and things seemed quiet. Then we came upon a crowd of people ahead of us being chased by police, who were obviously very uptight.

"The cops were calling people names and then some helmeted police started going over a guy. As you probably know, some two hundred working members of the press were out that night, and sixty of them were attacked. I saw a lot of this firsthand, so I know, as the commission report indicated, that the police were out of control, acting like individual hoodlums.

"We started to leave, but a squad car come down the street. Cops leaped out of the car with shotguns aimed at us. 'Get on home,' a cop said to me. 'That's what I'm trying to do,' I said. He hit me on the backside with his billy, and Feiffer and Lerner ran off in different directions.

"That police car was bristling, packed with angry men who were out for blood, out for fun. They were venting their frustrations over Vietnam, over race, and a bad press. They didn't know me; I wasn't being singled out. But what happened in Chicago could obviously have happened elsewhere.

And to anybody. My reaction was one of shock, incredulity. It all happened so quickly that there wasn't a chance for real fear."

He paused to light his pipe again. "I was left with a feeling of great sadness. Now we know the extent to which our society has become polarized. We don't have a leader like John Kennedy anymore, and if it comes to the nitty-gritty, the majority of the American people are ready to move to the right. I could see then when the majority of the people in Chicago and across the country wouldn't believe their own eyes—didn't want to believe what they saw. They sympathized with the police; people in the streets in Chicago actually booed TV news trucks. The intense reaction of people against what is happening on the campuses can easily become part of a larger anti-intellectual movement, bringing censorship, a 'back to God' drive, and an all-out effort to keep everyone in their place.

"And if there's repression in one area, it will occur in all. The people who voted for Wallace are uptight about everything that makes people free and happy. It's a real fascist thing of trying to take away the rights of other people and not let them enjoy the freedom of a democratic society."

Looking around the room seemed to reassure him—the large, round wooden table in the center; and behind him was a complete set of all the back issues of *Playboy*—including Vol. 1, No. 1, with its photograph of a nude Marilyn Monroe, for which he paid three hundred dollars and acquired the color separations—that almost filled a shelf across the entire length of a wall.

Naturally, one could not understand Hefner without taking a close look at *Playboy*, and this also meant going through that almost legendary running feature of recent American journalism, The Playboy Philosophy, which Hefner started writing in the December, 1962, issue and kept working at until 1965. Although far too long and maddeningly repetitive, the philosophy also has pages that crackle with a concern for human justice and an underlying idealism that cuts against the popular image of the archetypal "playboy." What was worth inquiry, however, was whether Hefner had basically revised his attitude on some of its key statements, in the light of recent events.

For example, in 1963 he had written:

> *If any of us were ever in serious doubt about the relative merits of group-oriented, collectivist socialism or communism versus self-oriented, individual initiative, free-enterprise capitalism, we've witnessed irrefutable evidence of the strengths and weaknesses of both over the last generation.... The mood is optimistic. In the Atomic Age, with the continuing threat of world conflict, no tomorrow can ever be a certainty, but certainty is a security the new generation does not require.... Many of the new generation are discovering that the ultimate satisfaction comes from living for both today and tomorrow.*

What about today, I asked him, after the assassinations, the Vietnam War and protests against it, the surfacing of black rage, the backlash, the growing polarization?

"Of course," he answered slowly, pausing after brief phrases, "as we're sitting here now we're looking at history on a very short-range basis. In the long run, however, there's still a real basis for optimism. The forces for social change are stronger than those against it.

"But what we're getting these days is a situation in which society at large is being placed above the individual and his rights. All this coming under the guise of law and order. If we were interested in the individual, we wouldn't be in Vietnam—and we'd be giving the Negro equal opportunity, instead of hollering about 'keeping them in line.'

"Socialism says in effect that society is more important than the individual; capitalism says the individual is important; but in our society today people can't compete equally, so you have to have some government controls. Socialism is a man working for the good of everybody else; capitalism is a man working for himself. Socialism is a political version of Christianity, but it just doesn't work well.

"I think we need a more socialized capitalism. Communism in Russia is becoming more capitalistic. Of course, we still have far more individual liberty in this country, and the middle class there doesn't enjoy the comforts we have. The real enemy is not communism but those forces here that undermine our democracy by separating the interests of the state from the interests of the individual people within it."

How did he feel necessary changes could be brought about?

"Kids now are falling into an antimaterialist mood. Many of them resent *Playboy* because it espouses the virtues of materialism. The real problem is to get the benefits of materialism to the most people possible. For example, Fidel Castro isn't the worst thing that ever happened to Cuba, but Cubans aren't nearly as well off as the majority of us can be in the United States if we work with what we have here. It's criminal that we still have people starving but we have less malnutrition and hunger than any other country in the world.

"This doesn't mean that the kids aren't right in complaining about some things—like the fact that eighty percent of our budget goes into the military. Usually the alternatives presented are either armament or disarmament. But the only real direction for the future is world government. Our basic mistake internationally is that after World War II we were not *for* democracy but *against* communism—again and again, winding up on the wrong side, as in Vietnam. We've got to find a way to establish a world government. There is no solution in continuing to arm *or* disarm; there has to be a world government which has the safeguards and controls."

In 1965 Hefner had written, "I think the area that will warrant the maximum consideration in the immediate future is this matter of personal identity: with a reevaluation and reemphasis of the importance of the individual; with society stressing the right of each of us to be different from one another, and fully recognizing the fact that this is, indeed, the very essence of what it means to be human." Reminded of these words during one of our evening sessions, he was quick to assert the same priority of concern. "Yes, that is the heart of the conflict going on now. There are so many things in our society that, by their progress, tend to dehumanize us. Like automation. If we aren't going to end up as in *1984*, it's going to be increasingly necessary to emphasize the human things.

"This means greater respect for the differences in man. Part of this struggle, of course, is the generation gap. There are far more men of goodwill under twenty-five than over. Young people should be treated as adults in every way at the age of eighteen; perhaps lowering the voting age would give them some sense of participation. But in any case everyone should do their own thing. Your own thing may not be mine, but I can respect you because you're doing yours."

Did Hefner extend this approach to recent demands for black separatism?

"I'm afraid," he frowned, "that some black militants are really helping the opposition. After all, racism is wrong when it comes from a black man, too. There are good and bad black men, good and bad white men. We have to get to the point where individuals are individuals."

I wanted to know how the individual would be able to establish a sense of his own identity.

"In the past, man got his basic idea of himself from his work. He was the doctor or cabinetmaker or farmer; this was his primary identity in the community. But for most people today work is so specialized and simplistic that it doesn't provide any ego gratification; you don't get to carry anything through to fruition. You're pushing a button on an assembly line or working on just one part of an advertising campaign.

"In the future, however, there will be more and more free time as the work schedule is shortened. Man will have to tackle new ways of establishing identity through avocations. He can't do it by being a TV watcher or a bowler."

Again I wondered aloud about Hefner's confidence in the future.

"We have the opportunity to establish a worldwide renaissance," he assured me with renewed energy. "But only if other problems are solved first. International law instead of warfare to control the possibilities of nuclear holocaust. An end to racism. An end to poverty around the world. The population explosion. The pollution of our natural resources. *Then,* all that remains is disease. If we spent our money on these things instead of war, by the year 2000 we could be moving into a real golden age. But it would still be a joyless world if science and technology become the masters, instead of we the masters of them.

"On the other hand, the final hour may be coming. We're going to have to find solutions to several problems on that list or be plummeted into a dark age. A person who, in the face of all our problems today, could think only of play and pleasure would be part of the enemy leading us down the road to destruction. But this doesn't mean that we shouldn't enjoy life to the fullest while working for worthwhile ends. We have to get beyond the guilts that go with pleasure. The idea that you lose spiritual values when you emphasize material things is wrong. The spirit is not separated from the body and the mind.

"There's nothing moral about us all becoming poor and sick and hungry. Morality ought to impel us to put an end to poverty and suffering and disease, and make the world a pleasant place to live in. But there's still so much guilt about materialism, like the old sexual guilts: 'Finish the food on your plate; people are starving in China.' People forget that it's materialism that has produced the best in education and research to end disease."

I reminded Hefner of another passage in The Playboy Philosophy in which he complained that traditional morality prized self-sacrifice above self-interest. "I'm frightened of the person who *thinks* he isn't self-involved," he burst out. "A man like Schweitzer, who ends up being very paternalistic and actually doing some harm. Oh, there's obviously a place for the Schweitzers. But others do far more for society than the men we canonize. If we could look into the past of those who have created the most for the world—geniuses like Michelangelo, Freud, the great scientists and inventors—I think we'd find out that they were not primarily other-directed. A person may be very self-involved—which is different from self-indulgent—and be caught up in creating a new beauty, discovering a new truth, and helping mankind. The man who invented the nail did more for the world than the guy who laid down on it.

"There's a real emotional danger in supposedly denying self. If you don't first like and respect yourself, how can you respect the rest of the world? Martyrdom is a very suspicious psychological set. I see parallels with our religious heritage that sees the road to heaven in a denial of the flesh, and living for other people rather than for yourself."

Talking with Hefner in The Mansion, amid all the reminders of spectacular success, increased my curiosity about the early days of *Playboy*. I could not help but look toward beginnings I did not know. When Hefner looked back, what did he remember and how did he see it? He must have felt an incredible buoyancy of spirit in November, 1953, when the first issue appeared and few professionals in the magazine business believed it would last more than a few months.

"I got a thousand from my folks," Hefner recalled with a smile. "And five hundred from somebody else. It even got down to tens from different people. But really, nothing can be learned about starting a magazine from our experience. We got such immediate response from readers, out of all proportion, and I think I understood fairly early the reason for this. A few years back a literary magazine ran an analysis comparing us with Benjamin Franklin and *Poor Richard's Almanac*. It pointed out that Franklin had developed an ethic for a Puritan period ['a penny saved is a penny earned'] while *Playboy* was concerned with what was needed now, an ethic for a society of leisure." ("It all happened so quickly," Richard Rosenzweig, Hefner's executive assistant, told me. "We're still trying to catch our breath. *Playboy* has been the single, spectacular American magazine publication in recent years. And, even in Europe, it's the largest-selling American magazine.")

We took the first issues down off the shelf and began thumbing through them together. It was fascinating how little of the original concept of the magazine had changed. "There's always been a high level of empathy between the magazine and its readers," Hefner enthused. "Maybe this is because I was very typical of my generation. My attitudes toward virginity and sex have great empathy with a wide range of young people who grew up at the same time. I was trying to put out a magazine for myself, one that I would enjoy reading. It described an urban world and the play and pleasure parts of life. If you had to sum up the idea of *Playboy*, it is anti-Puritanism. Not just in regard to sex, but the whole range of play and pleasure—you know, Puritanism outlawed the theater and many sporting events; it couldn't stand the idea that somewhere someone was having a good time.

"In a very real way, the thing that sets *Playboy* apart is the idea that sexual emancipation and female emancipation go hand in hand. The old Judeo-Christian concept kept women in slavery; they were seen as nonhuman, chattel. A woman's virginity was prized because, if she wasn't a virgin, she was used property. The criticism of *Playboy* as antifeminist is simplistic. For example, we ran a cartoon showing a guy trying to make out on the beach. The caption had him saying, 'Why talk about love at a time like this?' What we were doing, of course, was satirizing something that goes on all the time in our society, and hopefully decontaminating it.

"*Playboy* involves itself in sex and materialism. We're opposed to the idea that sex is either sacred or profane, not a normal part of living."

It was obvious that talking about the magazine made Hefner more expansive, and his enthusiasm even had him striding around the room. "Where we're unique is that we're directly related to what many people see as a part of their own identity. You don't find this in *Time* or *The New Yorker*. And who would walk around with a *Newsweek* tieclip or a *Life* golf-putter?"

I took advantage of a pause to offer a mildly deprecating comment about the banality of pinups. "Sure," Hefner conceded cheerfully, "they're very old-fashioned, but they represent an essential and healthy part of *Playboy*. The guys fighting over there in Vietnam are not of my generation—they're in their twenties and thirties—but it's very meaningful for them. Ours is the publication of *this* war—everything stops in camp when it arrives. You can tell how long a company has been in an area by the Playmates on the walls.

"Some magazines follow what they *think* kids are interested in. *Eye* presented rock groups, the psychedelic thing, Zen gurus, and all—and it went right into the toilet, *Esquire* stopped publishing cartoons because their editor said it was an editorial form no longer contemporary—bullshit. *Playboy* is doing better cartoons now than *Esquire* ever did."

But how could a recluse, locked up inside his mansion, stay sufficiently tuned in to new trends in order to guide the magazine?

"Magic is the answer," Hefner smiled. "Obviously, you have to keep the avenues of communication open. For example, I see all the films worth seeing. But there's the final thing, the intuitive ability to sort through the crap and find the nuggets. I'm awfully good at it, and I know it. Anyway, I'm an awfully good magazine editor for this particular magazine. *Playboy* wasn't any happy accident. Over the years, it did some things right that no other publication did. I have a lot of faith in my own gut-level feelings concerning the magazine."

When Hefner started *Playboy*, he thought of it as a journal of the younger generation; now he is older, and so is his magazine. It has, of course, achieved many of its objectives and called into being a host of imitators, but I knew that even some of its friends were asking whether it has "lost its cutting edge" and "become Establishment." Robert S. Preuss, *Playboy*'s business manager and circulation director partially conceded the point: "The world has simply caught up with us. We are victims of our own success." At the same time, he saw new markets opening up. "I see *Playboy* becoming more important worldwide. In the United States we don't have competition for the reader; we have imitators; in foreign countries, of course, imitators may tend to be competitors."

Hefner himself was unruffled when I raised the question during one of our postmidnight conversations. "*Playboy* is bedrock as a concept," he said firmly. "If you're publishing *Time*, you can always say let's publish one with pictures and call it *Life*, or one with sports and call it *Sports Illustrated*. What you get in *Time* can be replaced by TV; what you get in *Life* has already been replaced by TV. *Playboy*, however, goes right to the heart of what a great many people identify as who they are. It captures their dreams and aspirations; describes the world many of them want to be part of, and often are.

"That doesn't mean *Playboy* won't change. But our basic thing is about how to enjoy your leisure, and everything in our society is leading toward greater concern with what we're already involved with. Our importance may be even greater in the years ahead. After all, there's really only us and Grove Press, and they reach a much more limited audience. *Playboy* is like a Rorschach test. In twenty years, we will be viewed as one of the major elements of pop culture that influenced our time."

Hefner talked about changes in sexual mores. "Take stag films," he said by way of example, "they're still being made in motels, by guys without any artistic sense. But at least they have authenticity. And the nature of the activity has changed— previously, it was all a serving of the guy. Very little cunnilingus. Not much foreplay other than fellatio. The simple fact is that people aren't as uptight today. Sex itself has changed. Take my parents; they were incredibly typical of their generation. My mother and father were both farm people in Nebraska. Dad believed in the Horatio Alger bootstraps thing, and he did it. My mother was the only person on the block to give some sex education to kids, to the horror of the neighborhood. My brother and myself turned out to be, at least somewhat, sexually liberated. Of course, there are a number of things I know intellectually and yet there are still gaps in my relations with women.

"My parents gave me a lot, and yet there was a sense of suppression. Guilts were there, and a child is so sensitive to this, especially when their parents have sexual guilts. I'd have to say that my parents were extremely repressed, sexually, with all that this suggests. But of course, so was their entire generation. The idea of sex before marriage was wrong. Yes, my parents are very religious. They don't smoke. They don't drink. They don't swear. So in many ways it was my parents who, unintentionally, developed the iconoclastic rebellion in me."

A kindly, neat, gray-haired woman opened the door of a modest home on Chicago's West Side one afternoon and invited me inside. She had agreed to my coming but she was a bit guarded and reserved toward a new stranger, yet her natural candor, warmth, and outgoing spirit were soon manifest: it was Grace Hefner, Hugh Hefner's mother. She led me into the cluttered middle-class living room of the house where Hugh and his brother, Keith, had been reared; I made myself comfortable in an easy chair, and she sat on the couch.

"When Hugh was young, he was an early riser but he needed a lot of sleep," Mrs. Hefner told me. "He took naps even when he was going to kindergarten at four-and-a-half, which is one of the mistakes we made with him. You see, this meant that he went with the older children and he felt sort of inferior. I remember him coming home once and asking, 'How do you skip?' The older children met in the morning and the younger ones in the afternoon. So we wanted him to go in the morning because of his nap. He didn't develop physically—skating, things of that sort—as quickly as his younger brother did.

"When he was quite small, about two, he was very outgoing and at ease with anyone he met. Then we moved into a flat where the landlady said it would be all right to play in the backyard, but made him feel uncomfortable. He couldn't understand that she was very nervous, and from then on, he met folks with a reserve. He wasn't sure how he would be treated.

"We moved here when Hugh was just four. He really lived here most of his growing-up time. We bought this place because we felt the children would be less hampered. This area wasn't built up, then; very few houses and back of us was mostly prairie. There were meadowlarks and snakes. I'm sure he told you he liked to play with animals.

"And he was fortunate with the youngsters he grew up with. None of them tried to dominate the others. There were two other families in particular, each had two boys, and the six of them usually played here on our back porch. We had an old table and they also used an old desk as a platform. They used to make clay figures and ships, and they'd act out stories which they made up."

Mrs. Hefner brought coffee without losing the thread of her memories. "Hugh never was particularly active in athletics because he wasn't very good at it. They played football on the prairie sometimes, but he didn't take much part in school athletics."

She showed me boyhood pictures of Hugh, pointing out that he had always looked thin. "But when he was working so hard a few years ago he was so gaunt, almost a skeleton. When Glenn, my husband, and I would be down to see him, I'd try to take some pictures, in order to keep a record. I have quite a collection, you know. And once, I took one of these pictures to Hugh and said, 'See? You look ghastly. You'd better be careful.' "

His mother paused and looked out the window. It was absolutely quiet in the house, and her delivery always remained calm and controlled.

"Hugh was always very sensitive to other people and I'm sure he hasn't outgrown it. For example, in the first grade, his teacher was very old-fashioned, almost a martinet. Children learned things: that's all there was to it. She was severe about any infractions of the rules. Once, when he had come home to lunch, he said he didn't want to go back. It was the sense of discord in the classroom. He felt sorry for the children in the room who were being called down. But I remember the mother of one of the girls in that same class said to me, 'It didn't bother my daughter at all. She knew her lesson. She just was glad that it wasn't her who was being bawled out.'

"I always tried to make my boys see that when a child was mean he was unhappy. But you couldn't always tell what was making Hugh feel unhappy, because he was very much a loner.

"He never seemed to be too interested in others up through the eighth grade. Of course, he did have friends. He was interested in a little Jewish girl in the fourth or fifth grade. On Valentine's Day, he had a card for her and was home from school with a cold. He wanted to know if I would deliver it to her father. I did. The father took it and just smiled. I remember how, one time, another boy in school had insulted her Jewishness. There weren't many Jewish families in this area, and the prejudiced attitudes bothered Hugh and Keith a lot.

"The first girl Hugh liked—she wouldn't even look at him. He was so disappointed, and then she moved away."

(Hefner remembered the girl: "All the guys in class loved her. There's always that class beauty. She had long blonde curls . . . you know a magazine writer once said that my adjustment to girls was difficult in my adolescent years, that it was fantasy intstead of reality. He said I collected butterflies, made me seem almost effeminate. In fact I collected animals, but was mostly interested in drawing cartoons. Let's see; I started dating at thirteen, and went steady twice in high school.")

Mrs. Hefner continued to tell me her son's story: graduation from high school, January, 1944; enlistment (age seventeen) in the army in March. "The prejudice thing came up again during special training," she recalled. "He even wrote home that he was grateful we had taught him to judge people as individuals. Apparently he had dated a Jewish girl and some other fellows in his dormitory commented on it. Keith ran into it, too, when he was a pledge in a fraternity at Northwestern and they tried to tell him whom he could date. He was blackballed and had to get out of the fraternity."

I tried to balance the tolerance Hefner had learned at home with his statement that his parents had developed rebellion in him because of the atmosphere of suppression. I paraphrased his comment and Mrs. Hefner only smiled, her voice remaining as calm and mild as before. "Oh yes, we *were* very strict," she conceded. "I always had a strong sense of duty—you know, this should be done because it was the right thing to do. But I at least tried to explain *why*. They had to go to bed because, as I told them, this was the time for growing. They went to bed to get their nine hours. Their little playmates didn't have to, so this was a hardship for them. I got a lot of ideas and books about bringing up children from a trained friend.

"Let's see—I didn't believe in going to movies on Sunday. The other four boys they played with—two Catholics and two Lutherans—they had no rules about this, and they went to shows on Sunday, so naturally this was a sore point.

"Also, because of family tragedies due to drinking, we never served it. Frankly, we didn't want the boys to drink. When Hugh was in the army, he wrote back, 'I just had my first taste of wine. But don't worry: it was just Episcopal Holy Communion.'" (Hefner didn't remember this, and explained later, "It was probably because of a girl I was going with who happened to be Episcopalian.")

Grace Hefner smoothed her dress and went on. "He probably thought of us as prudish. But what we did was perfectly natural in terms of our own upbringing. You have to look at what a person felt at *that* time as opposed to what a person might feel now.

"At least we always tried to answer their questions truthfully. We even carried this to the point of not having any Santa Claus. Hugh and Keith understood their Christmas presents came from family and friends. There was even a little difficulty for them with their young friends about this, but I don't think we spoiled their holidays at all. Christmas was always good, and at Easter they hid eggs. When he was in the army, Hugh came home on leave at Easter; he was very tired. But Keith, who was still only fifteen, called up to his brother, 'Come on down and help find the Easter eggs,' and he came down. They seemed to have a real good time. And that was the last Easter hunt."

I asked Mrs. Hefner about her sons' religious upbringing.

"Our rules were not just for their physical well-being but spiritual as well," she replied. "We insisted they go to Sunday school. There wasn't any nearby church. My husband got very active in the men's class in the adult Sunday school at a Methodist church. Later, when Hugh was about sixteen, they tried to organize a Methodist church in this neighborhood, and Hugh and I would go to church together. The minister was an older man who had almost retired; he mostly just reminisced about his own life.

"When Hugh was going to Sunday school, he said he never got anything out of what they were saying except for one man, someone he could argue with. But this man apparently was not a very good scholar, so occasionally Hugh was able to stump him with questions.

"We didn't have family prayers, formal devotions, and all that, but I'd say we were religious in that we judged our actions by what we thought we should do according to our religious upbringing." She made it seem neither apology nor self-justification.

We had more coffee and I amused her by describing the stacks of papers I had seen all over The Mansion—on the floor of her son's bedroom, private quarters, and office. "A mess, isn't it?" she sighed. "He hasn't changed. When he'd be back here from school in Illinois, he'd bring all his things into the dining room, and his bedroom was always papered with Petty girls."

Her smile broadened. "I have such happy memories of their childhood. Until Hugh was ten, they shared a room with a double-bed. They had a big clay table and would play together for hours. They used nut picks for spears when they were whale fishers or savages, and the clay objects were full of holes." ("That was for shooting," Hefner explained later; "you'd shake the dice to see if the object was mortal, if it lived or not.")

"They were both trustworthy; I never had to hide things from them. Of course, I was a disciplinarian; they knew what they could touch. But I always allowed them to have their friends here and we tried to be democratic about things.

"Because of the friend I mentioned, the one who had given me books on child development, I would try to answer a question about sex if the kids on the block asked me. One mother in the neighborhood was upset and called me up. She told me that God should have arranged things better, and that she wished children could be born without sex."

I told Mrs. Hefner that Hugh had commented on how sensitive a child was to a sense of guilt in regard to sex.

"Well, my parents never discussed sex with me," she said. "I was told nothing at all. So it was quite a step for me to be honest at all. I realized later that I had said nothing to the boys about emotions—just this is thus-and-so. It never entered my mind—it wasn't in the book, and that was that. But you have to consider the kind of training I had. I thought I was progressive.

"Hugh tells me now 'You were overly modest.' My husband was probably more so than I. Glenn never wanted me to wear powder and rouge. The boys saw their teachers at school wearing it and asked me about it. I said, 'Father doesn't want me to wear it.' Then one night I was going out to a P.T.A. meeting to raise money, and I thought 'I'll just paint myself up outrageously, and we'll see how queer it looks.' But the boys said, 'Mother, you're beautiful.' I took it off as soon as I got to the meeting.

"The truth is the boys didn't get enough time with their father. Not that it was Glenn's fault; the aluminum company where he was an accountant was expanding and he had to work overtime. Before the depression he didn't get home until eleven or twelve o'clock every night. Even during the depression he worked late, and Saturdays too. He would take us to the movies Saturday night, after he got home around four or five o'clock. The boys would know him on Saturday night and Sunday. Other mornings he would get up before they were awake. He wouldn't let me get up to make breakfast."

One knew a great deal about the Hefners from the simple style in which they lived, even though their son would have been glad to provide them with luxury. Mr. Hefner still worked as an accountant, but was now employed by *Playboy* as the company treasurer. "Possessions don't mean much to us," Mrs. Hefner explained. "I've tried to do what I should, according to my religious beliefs. And I feel guilty about having so much when others have so little. I feel the same way about the buildings and possessions of the church. Is is right, really? When we had young ministers and their wives as guests in our house, I used to ask them, 'Was the church doing what is right about its own wealth?' They didn't know the answer."

Her son's fame had obviously not disturbed Grace Hefner's sense of her own identity. "If anyone asks, 'Oh, are you Hugh's mother?'—I remember being introduced to someone like that at a fancy restaurant—my answer is, 'Is that the only reason I'm important?' But it doesn't bother me. I don't have any driving need to do this or that.

"When Hugh was a senior in high school—it was during the war—there was a question of drafting women. I thought, well, if they needed women, I'd do what I could. I worked during the war and continued for eighteen years, retiring at sixty-five. Then I started calling on the shut-ins of our church. When I was seventy, Glenn and the boys bought a car for me, and I learned to drive.

"As for the magazine, our close friends differ about it. Some won't let it inside their homes; others read it every month and seem to like it. It's not something I would read and be interested in, but I respect Hugh because he believes in what he's doing.

"Perhaps he's too self-centered to have a family," she suggested. "But the world would be the loser if there weren't folks who dig into their interests to the exclusion of all else. Hugh has a strong moral sense about what a person should do. While I don't agree with many things, I've always respected his honesty. Even when Hugh was growing up, he was always so intense he'd be miserable if he couldn't do the thing he wanted. I was rather fearful for him in that sense."

Had he, I asked, done the thing that he wanted?

"I hope so," she said.

After my conversation with Mrs. Hefner, it was quite understandable that Hefner was by no means simply rejecting his childhood, even though he was critical of some aspects of his upbringing. One curious incident that he did bring up, however, involved a favorite toy that he had when he was four or five years old. "It was a blanket—like a security blanket. The blanket had bunnies on it and was called the bunny blanket. I also had a dog, a wire-haired terrier; they gave it to me when I got out of the hospital after a mastoid operation. I loved that little dog, so I gave him the blanket. But he'd been sick and died a few days afterward, and the blanket was burned."

I asked his mother about the blanket, but her recollection was somewhat different. "The blanket wasn't Hugh's at all—it was really given to Keith, I believe. When we gave Hugh a dog, he was very ill with a mastoid operation. Then he had his tonsils and adenoids removed. I remember one evening when two fine doctors came to look at him: he was sitting there with this piece of cotton in his hands, talking to it and making it talk to him. We bought him the dog when he came home from the hospital; we didn't realize it was ill. When it died, Hugh wrapped it in this blanket and they had a funeral out on the prairie. Then we burned the blanket. The boys dug the puppy up a little later to see if it was still there. Hugh only had the dog a few weeks, so he couldn't have been *too* attached to it."

Even after hearing what his mother had said, Hefner insisted on his own version. "The blanket was in *my* bed and it was *mine*," he told me. "I gave it to the dog specifically because it had such meaning to me. And I was very upset when we had to burn it. Of course, it's important only as a kind of curiosity. Actually, this whole blanket business came out for the first time about twelve years ago, in the early days of the magazine, when we all took a psychological test. The bunny is the key; you put the two things together and you go wild."

Playboy editor Spectorsky warned me against making too much of the incident. "I don't think Hef would have thought about the blanket if he hadn't seen Orson Welles's *Citizen Kane*. Even though he's very independent in his thinking, he's also very suggestible. You remember the sled, bearing the name 'Rosebud,' which Welles sets up in the audience's mind as the answer to the mystery of Kane's life? Well, after that movie, I'm sure that Hef had to find his own Rosebud, and it turned out to be the blanket."

When I told Hefner what Spectorsky had said, however, Hefner pointed out an important difference between the bunny blanket and the sled: "In *Citizen Kane*, Rosebud represented the life the hero *didn't* live. It reflected the lost man he might have been. But there's no parallel in my case—I followed my own direction in life. Rosebud meant an opportunity lost; the bunny blanket is simply a curious, remarkable detail out of my past."

Hefner was discharged from the army in April, 1946, and entered the University of Illinois that fall, graduating in two and a half years "by working summers and doubling up." Robert S. Preuss, who roomed with him for a year at Illinois, is now business manager and circulation director of *Playboy*. "I'm just a Polish bookkeeper," he told me, laughing. Amiable and easygoing, he clearly shares some of the more serious elements of Hefner's basic attitude. "I suppose all of us at the magazine feel the same way," he mused, "that there should be self-choice. This is where what Hef is doing is significant. I'm an ex-Catholic, for example. I feel it's wrong for Catholics to say to everyone, '*This* is religion.' And the same principle holds for sex laws: there should be self-choice for adults. Everything Hef says goes back to this point."

Several people had suggested to me that Hefner was going through a period of personal transition, but Preuss saw no evidence of this. "I see him not in transition but doing more of the same. And he still has a pulse for what is going on because of the people he sees. The only thing that's really changed is that cards have taken the place of the typewriter." He was referring to the fact that Hefner had stopped writing The Playboy Philosophy and now often stayed up all night in The Mansion playing cards with friends. "Pounding the typewriter on The Philosophy was more of a bad habit than anything else. A striving for personal identity, not only a striving, but a kind of desperation.

"We didn't live in a fraternity at Illinois, just an organized house called the Granada Club, with two guys in a room. You know, a myth has been built up about Hefner but not in him. I've noticed this, for example, when I'll bring up someone who used to live with us at the Granada. I'll say, 'Hef, you remember that guy who lived in the corner room?' He usually remembers, and much more than I'd expect. But there are some situations he disremembers; certain people become just employees. You can tell by bringing around guys from different periods: the guy from college, he remembers; someone from two years ago, maybe he'll ask, 'Who was that?'

"I'm a C. P. A., had my own firm. But in fifty-nine he asked me to sell out and join him, and after much soul-searching, I did. The reason we saw each other after college was our wives; all four of us knew each other."

Had Hefner changed?

"He's much the same guy in all the little things—in what he likes, what he laughs at, and so forth. I get as fucking frustrated playing gin with him today as I used to get playing cards with him in college. And he's just as slow today. But, of course, he's different in terms of money. I don't mean that's bad—hell, we were poor, living on the G. I. bill. Things you used to run out and do yourself, now you sit down and say, 'Hey, where are they?' The extent of this surprises me in myself, much less in him—after all, he's rich; in comparison, I'm a pauper. He's the employer, I'm an employee, but we don't have a barrier between us."

Four months after graduation from the University of Illinois, Hefner married Mildred Williams.

"We went steady through college and then got married," Hefner told me. "There's the assumption in some quarters that Hefner got married, started the magazine, was surrounded by beautiful girls, and ended the marriage. In fact, it ended because two people were immature and unprepared for marriage."

He cleaned out his pipe thoughtfully before continuing. "At first we lived in the house above my folks. Later we moved to the south side of Chicago into our own apartment, where the first couple of issues of the magazine were published— 6052 South Harper. Both of the kids were born there, Christie Ann and David." The girl is now sixteen, the boy thirteen. There was a divorce in 1959, and Hefner's ex-wife has remarried and lives with her family in Chicago; Hefner sees his two children regularly.

The details of his early career were reviewed with obvious relish.

"At college I hadn't wanted to take the so-called practical things in journalism, so I majored in psychology, with courses in creative writing, art, and sociology. And of course, afterward I couldn't get a job on any Chicago paper.

"My first job was with a carton company, interviewing for their personnel department. I worked there from April to September, 1949—forty-five dollars a week. The bigotry in their hiring practices really bothered me: they didn't want to hire Jews or blacks or anyone with a long name.

"I quit. During the end of that year I tried drawing cartoons. I created two different comic strips—'Fred Frat,' about my college days, and 'Gene Fantas, Psycho-Investigator,' about a psychologist-detective. I was good at the writing, but not at the art. Actually, I drew some cartoons for *Playboy* in the first issues, but later my editorial role forced me to reject my own artwork.

"In the winter and spring of 1950 I studied at Northwestern and wrote a paper on sex behavior and the law for a graduate course in sociology. There are interesting connections between my conclusions in that paper and what I wrote in the magazine years later. I compared the sex statutes throughout the country with actual sex practices, as indicated by Kinsey. My conclusions were, as you might guess, the same permissive, humanistic views I expressed later in The Philosophy: that there should be a distinction between law and morality—that is, a separation between Church and State. It all seems commonplace and obvious today, but the professor gave me two grades—A for my research, B+ because of my conclusions. Yet my conclusions were the same, in essence, as those of the American Law Institute for its model penal code, and close to those of the Wolfenden Report in Britain."

As important as this paper would prove as a guide to Hefner's message to society, he was impatient with the idea of more school and became increasingly intrigued with the idea of a starting a magazine, perhaps about Chicago, perhaps a trade magazine for cartoonists. In June, 1950, he got his first writing job as a copywriter for Carson, Pirie, Scott, the Chicago department store, at forty dollars a week. "I had an office of my own," he smiled, "although it didn't have a door on it."

In January, 1951, Hefner went to *Esquire*. "They were looking for a copywriter in the promotion department, to write renewal letters and solicit subscriptions by mail. I got sixty dollars a week. A year later they moved the promotion and circulation department to New York and offered me a cost of living increase based on the economic differentials there. But when I asked for a five-dollar-a-week raise, I was refused.

"Then I produced a book of cartoons called 'That Toddlin' Town,' a dollar paperback that sold in bookstores. It made a small profit and nice publicity.

"I got a job at Publishers' Development Corporation at eighty dollars a week. They put out a bunch of small magazines, from grade school art magazines to a photography book with nudes. I sold magazines promotionally to newsstands, and also got valuable experience in selling by mail; when I started *Playboy*, I had had direct contact with newsstand people and also was familiar with the problems of selling anything by mail.

"I went next to 'Children's Activities,' a popular children's magazine. I was promotion-circulation manager at one hundred and twenty a week. I created an entire direct-mail campaign—you do a renewal series of perhaps five or six letters, to go out a few weeks before expiration of subscriptions. I used cartoons of little animals with plastic tears pasted on them.

"More and more, though, while I was learning in all these jobs, I realized that I wouldn't be happy until I was on my own. So I left that fall (1952) to start *Playboy*."

By 1954 the magazine was sufficiently established for Hefner to move it out of his apartment on Chicago's south side to its first real office at 11 East Superior Street. "It was across from Holy Name Cathedral," Hefner recalled. "There's a dress shop now in what used to be my office. The people behind us, they made prayer benches. You know, I took a walk over there last year and went through our old place.

"Pretty soon we took one whole floor, then two floors, and soon the whole building. And finally two or three floors in other buildings close by. Then, after four or five years, we moved to 232 East Ohio, taking over three or four floors, and later, other space in buildings in the area.

"I was living at 232 in a little bedroom at the back. Actually, I had another apartment but never lived in it; in fact, I never finished furnishing it. Used to wander around the office in my pajamas. Then, when I bought The Mansion, I brought my work over here. Now I can shut out outside interference from staff members and others, and work at my own pace."

Playboy was obviously a unique meeting of a man and an idea, but even after all that Hefner had told me, much of the dynamics of the magazine's operation seemed mysterious. There was no way to explain its success in a formula, but Anson Mount, the intense, brooding, but eternally smiling public affairs manager of the magazine provided additional insight by calling attention to the way in which Hefner chose his associates. "Some people say Hef's a genius," Mount told me one day over coffee. "Well, if he has one talent that's seen him through, it's his ability to judge character and spot who will be useful. His lieutenants are a study in themselves. One played violin in the Indianapolis Symphony; one had an inherited job in a company his father owned; another sang in a Gilbert and Sullivan traveling troupe; another played trumpet in a jazz band.

"I was a cabdriver up from the South and won a short-story contest. Then I got sick and was in bed in a veteran's hospital when Hef saw my story and liked it. When I got out, I went to see him at his office. 'When would you like to go to work?' he asked. Not 'would you like to' but 'when.' Salary wasn't even discussed. I started immediately. I didn't know anything about publishing or public relations.

"You see," he explained, "Hef has confidence in us, and he doesn't mind criticism—in his living room or in print. He's only wary of personal confrontation with his critics in public. For example, he's only spoken at colleges three times—all in May, 1965. I traveled with him in a Lear jet. We left Chicago one afternoon at four, he was talking at Cornell, and we were back home at midnight. He also went to Johns Hopkins and North Carolina, then he stopped—his curiosity had been satisfied.

"But as far as the magazine is concerned, the main thing was that he was able to choose basically bright enthusiastic people who could learn empirically. You know what he said recently? 'If I knew then what I know now, I wouldn't have tried.' "

I told Spectorsky what Mount had said; he smiled and drove home the main point of the lesson. "Let's face it," he said, "if Hefner had taken the *Playboy* idea to New York, it would never have started. Fortunately, he learned long ago that all those experts—with a capital E—are full of shit."

Critics, of course, want to explain the success of *Playboy* in terms of a simple exploitation of sex—which, indeed, is synonymous with the magazine, and also with Hefner, in the public consciousness. The truth is much more complex, and Hefner is much too serious about the subject for this explanation to be very helpful. For example, during my conversations with Hefner I referred to an incident that occurred not long before at Grinnell College when a representative of the magazine spoke to the students. Apparently several students, male and female, had stripped naked to protest *Playboy*'s alleged exploitation of women and sex; when they asked the *Playboy* representative to join them in corporate nudity, he declined.

"Ten years ago, without *Playboy*, those students would have been too embarrassed to take their clothes off in public to protest anything," he retorted. "We've played a decontaminating role in changing attitudes toward nudity. Why, fifteen years ago, a young man would have been embarrassed to look at a picture of a nude girl if a girl were sitting beside him.

"The feminists who criticize us don't realize how *Playboy*, far more than the women's magazines, is responsible for the nongirdle look, the bikini, the miniskirt, the openness to nudity. *Vogue* has nudes now, with nipples—some good nudes. Ten years ago we ran a feature, 'The Nude Look'—it was a parody on 'The New Look,' and we made dresses out of cellophane."

I reminded Hefner of the concern he had expressed (The Playboy Philosophy, July, 1963) over the tendency to reduce the differences between the sexes. "I'm not as worried as I used to be," he commented. "The trend has increased, but it has both positive and negative aspects. What I was complaining about was the so-called idealization of women in the women's magazines, which in fact expressed a very antisexual bias. The female mannequin was very tall, trussed up in a girdle, flat-chested and angular. Of course, we've now got the word 'unisex' in the language; maybe it's part of the identity crisis we're having today.

"There ought to be room for a wide range in individual sexual expression, but I can't agree that there should be no differences between male and female, emotionally and psychologically. I'm glad that female emancipation has moved ahead, and it's right to relate it to Negro emancipation. But still, there *is* a difference. Let's put it this way: I would like not to be aware of a person as Negro or white, blond or brown. But I don't want to be unaware of male or female. We must allow the widest range of what it means to be masculine or feminine, sure. However, after you announce the truly human, then you must announce male or female—it's basic to the question of identity."

The very extent of his defense suggested that Hefner had been stung by criticism from advocates of women's liberation. "*Playboy*'s been on the side of humanity and reason in all the causes that are important," he insisted, "so you'd think that female emancipators would separate their friends from their enemies. We've helped their movement in several ways. And after all, woman has the vote; she can hold property; she gets more than a square deal in divorce laws; and she's taken great strides forward economically. The major strides ahead are of a sexual nature, like abortion, and undermining the surviving social attitudes that there are only virgins and nonvirgins, good girls and bad girls. But we can't ignore the fact that there also exist a large number of competitive females who are trying to castrate the guys they come in contact with because they're unhappy with the whole male-female relationship. They're out to show how impotent the male is, in conversation, in bed, or a thousand other ways. Instead of a love relationship, it becomes a hostile war of the sexes."

I was reminded of a sentence that he had written in the sixth installment of The Playboy Philosophy: "It has long seemed quite incredible—indeed, incomprehensible—to us that detailed descriptions of murder, which we consider a crime, are acceptable in our art and literature, while detailed descriptions of sex, which is not a crime, are prohibited. It is as though our society puts hate above love—favored death over life." We had come to the end of one of our sessions, and I couldn't help wondering what the Yale boy and the Vassar girl who had sneered at *Playboy* back in New Haven would have thought as Hefner sought to bring the evening to a proper conclusion. "The major civilizing influence in the world isn't religion," he said, "it's sex. If we were all one sex, there would be all hostility and no creation. There wouldn't even be the little love we have on the planet now."

Perhaps some of Hefner's enjoyment of his spectacular success lay in his continuing awareness of the difficulties of growing up. "As a teenager," he assured me, "I was very outgoing, very busy in activities. Even earlier, when I was just a kid, I started a one-penny neighborhood paper; I typed it up myself and sold it to neighbors. In the sixth grade, I started what became the school paper, called *The Pepper;* when my wife went back, years later, as a substitute teacher, the paper was still going.

"And did you know, we had a reunion of our eighth-grade class at The Mansion about three years ago? It was fascinating—there were about thirty kids in the class, and about twenty-seven showed up; one guy called all the way from California. I wondered beforehand, since our worlds are so different now, what will we have to talk about? But it was great.

"But I guess the last two years in high school were the happiest of my life—until the magazine started. The time between college and when I started *Playboy*, no, things didn't work out, either on the home front or in my work. In high school I had established success in terms of extracurricular activities and in boy-girl relations. But later, until *Playboy*, I never could quite get the chance to express myself as a human being, either in one-to-one relationships or in my work."

Hefner expressed little bitterness about the past, however, except in the area of religion, which, I told him, seemed to have affected his life as profoundly as any bishop of my acquaintance. "Yes, I'm still reacting," he admitted. "My iconoclasm and anti-establishment attitudes have probably grown out of a response to the church as inhuman and irrational.

"I remember very well having an argument in grammar school with a fundamentalist Sunday-school teacher. In general, I was less angry than bored. Some place along the way, I simply decided the whole idea of God, heaven, and hell was pure fancy.

"When I was in high school, I was able to make an arrangement to go to a Sunday evening Sunday school with my girl friend. I never joined the church, though, and to be fair, I was never forced to. They didn't practice infant baptism and I just decided not to be baptized.

"Later, in college, I did a short play for a writing class, on the effects of a scientific discovery proving that there was no God. The final resolution was the suppression of the information because the people could not live with such knowledge. The instructor, however, told me that the play wasn't relevant, because everybody already knew there was no God or any system of absolutes."

Most of what Hefner was to tell me concerning religion during our sessions at The Mansion had already been stated in the fourth installment of The Playboy Philosophy, written in 1963:

"Religion is based upon faith; democracy is based upon reason. America's religious heritage stresses selflessness, subservience to a great Power and the paying of homage to Him in long-established, well-defined, well-organized ways; democracy teaches the importance of self, a belief in one's self and one's own abilities. Religion teaches that man should live for others; our democracy's free-enterprise system is based on the belief that the greatest good comes from men competing with one another. Religion offers a special blessing to the meek and the promise that they will inherit the earth; democracy requires that men speak out and be heard.

"Most religion in America teaches that man is born with the stain of Original Sin upon him; a free democracy stands on the belief that man is born innocent and remains so until changed by society. Most organized religion in the U.S. is rooted in a tradition that links man's body with evil, physical pleasures with sin, and pits man's mind and soul against the devil of the flesh; the principles underlying our democracy recognize no such conflict of body, mind and soul. Religion tends to de-emphasize material things, discourage a concern over the acquisition of wealth, bless the poor and promise that they shall dwell with God in the Kingdom of Heaven; our free-enterprise system is founded on the ideal that striving to materially better oneself is worthwhile and benefits not only the individual, but the world around him.

Most religions are based upon the importance of the next world; democracy is based upon the importance of this one."

I asked Hefner why, in his opinion, organized religion in the West had tended to be antisexual.

"Christianity took a nonhumanistic attitude from the dualism of St. Paul," he answered. "Of course, you can work out some after-the-fact rationale for this. At the time families and nations were dependent on the number of offspring for strength in an agrarian society. Young men were needed to fight the wars. All this helped emphasize sex exclusively as procreation.

"They were afraid of enjoyment, maybe because Christianity started as a religion that suffered. And it came out of a Judaism that suffered. In the Middle Ages, of course, life was even lousier than before. And remember, in all of this, the people were told over and over that they have been conceived in sin.

"Later, when America was born, there was a wringing of hands: 'They're not ready to rule themselves,' the old guard said. But how do you get ready to be free? You learn. You acquire responsibilities. Christianity, however, says man is weak, the devil is in the flesh. So, all pleasures become suspect, and man ends up relying on divine magic instead of his own initiative."

Today Hefner rules over an immense empire; he explained it to me as a privately held series of corporations. "It's hard to estimate exact net worth. We made sixteen million in two corporations this year before taxes. My personal wealth consists of eighty-one per cent of the H. M. H. Publishing Company, Inc., and seventy-nine per cent of Playboy Clubs International, Inc., which includes my share of the stock owned by H. M. H."

In addition to the magazine and the clubs, there are now hundreds of Playboy products, a movie theater in Chicago, a modeling agency, a new airplane, and The Playboy Press. ("We're just getting started with two dozen titles and we're thinking about going into the book club business.")

Hefner was delighted by the diversity of the operation. "The name, Playboy, indicates a concept that has broadened into much, much more. We have our own flag and bunny army. Playboy is a world unto itself, a world within a world. It's inconceivable that I could ever sell the company—it would be like selling a loved one, or myself. It's my own identity, what I want to be and accomplish."

He became more expansive as he tried to suggest all the implications of his idea. "All these Playboy products and clubs—they're simply extensions of the reality of what the magazine represents. An urban setting. Night-time activity. Attention to beautiful girls. Comfort. Many people bring their own view of *Playboy* and of themselves to the clubs; some see everything there through that view and leave happily. But the final ingredient of the clubs is intangible, an aura; any successful restaurant or club is more than its food and decor. There's a spirit. And because of the magazine, we can continue to keep the concept fresh, month after month, year after year, as it becomes more and more popular."

The same philosophy has led Hefner and the magazine to set up a Playboy Foundation, which he described as its social-activist arm. "We're concerned about sex education, trying to change abortion laws (the present backlash, and the 'suppressive legislation' on sex still on the books in many states"). Hefner's personal involvement in this area, one will recall, goes back to the term paper he did at Northwestern after he got out of the army. These antiquated sex laws would be overturned, he claimed, if the public saw them universally applied. But enforcement is capricious, usually "against someone who looks a little different, or belongs to the wrong race, or has wrong ideas. They're constantly talking about sodomy, but that seems to mean whatever there are social taboos against. But whenever people start legislating against 'a crime against nature,' it really means that they think all sex is bad except coitus for procreation. Sodomy laws are as crazy as drug laws. There are penalties of twelve, fourteen, and twenty years for oral and anal intercourse, whether homosexual or heterosexual, or even between husband and wife. In one case the Foundation handled, a guy had had anal intercourse with his wife; she had given her permission, but he was sentenced to something like fourteen years. We questioned the constitutionality of the law and got him out on a technicality."

It was hard to reconcile Hefner's crusading urge with his celebrated circular bed or the five-and-a-half-million-dollar airplane he had ordered. "Well," he said, smiling indulgently at my comment, "I spend many hours in that bed; I enjoy it tremendously—and the plane, it's basically for convenience. A certain number of things you do add a style to living. After all, we could get by in overalls, but when we wear a suit that makes a statement about who we are. I didn't think about the bed or the plane and say, 'This will be great publicity,' but I must somehow have realized they would fit the image I had of myself and the world has of me. Both consciously and subconsciously, I relate a personal image to things. And I confess I enjoy the public mystique that exists around me—yes, even more than the money."

I asked about his TV show, "Playboy After Dark," mentioning that Spectorsky had felt it wasn't up to Hefner's standards. "Well," he explained, "when I did 'Playboy's Penthouse' ten years ago, my motivation was to reach a wider public. At the time, *Playboy* still had an image problem; it was important to show people that I didn't have horns, and that the magazine wasn't just a dirty book. This time I was primarily interested in being forced to change my lifestyle— you know, stop taking amphetamines, put on a little weight, and get out of the house. And what we're trying to do with the show is potentially interesting and entertaining. The television screen is small, so you ought to present variety in an intensely personal way; we're trying to use the camera as a third person at our party. I expected to be buried by the critics, but when *Daily Variety* re-reviewed the show—the one with Sammy Davis—they raved, and suggested that our new, more casual approach might become a trend. Don't forget our budget is only about thirty thousand dollars, very low for a major night-time show."

Nor did Hefner feel at all defensive about the Playboy clubs. At his encouragement, I had even gone out to inspect the Playboy club-resort at Lake Geneva, Wisconsin, which had cost ten million dollars, had the largest private airport in the country, and had surely earned the ancient promotional epithet of "spectacular"; I agreed with Hefner that it was "a Disneyland for adults." But what, I asked, about the criticism that Playboy clubs simply encourage voyeurism—look, but don't touch?

He shrugged his shoulders. "Sure, I know, it isn't real life. And they complain because the bunnies in the clubs are protected by the rules. I guess they think the Playboy club is supposed to be Orgy-city. Let's face it; people have to go after us because we're involved in challenging the two greatest guilts our society has: materialism and sex.

"I'm glad we're in that fight and proud that it's the most successful nightclub operation of all time—nineteen clubs now, and we're in London, Montreal, Jamaica, and still spreading. But we've done a few other things, too; we started the black comics, for instance—Dick Gregory was the first Negro comic to be booked in a white circuit. And we have black bunnies in all the clubs, including those in the South. In New Orleans and Miami, we had to buy back the clubs from franchise owners because of racial discrimination.

"The clubs are an extra dimension of the magazine; they represent the communication of my views and tastes and interests relevant to these changing times. And you don't get clipped; the clubs aren't in the hands of hoodlums. We keep bringing up young talent, give it a chance to get some training.

"Of course, some people still see the bunny costume as degrading—to me, it's simply a uniform identifying an occupation, like a nurse's or stewardess's garb. You've seen them here at The Mansion—the bunnies are a cross section of American girls. Bunnies, and the bunny dormitory here, are like the round bed in my room: that little inner voice, my sixth sense, told me that they would fit into the image people wanted to have of me."

Barbara Klein, the new romance in Hefner's life, visited The Mansion for several days during my stay there. Nineteen years old, she had gone to high school in Sacramento, and attended college at UCLA; it was her photograph that graced the July, 1969, and March, 1970, covers of *Playboy*. Barbara —who preferred being called Barbi "because it's a name that doesn't belong to anyone else"—was certainly lovely, but with all the girls around him, it was hard to understand what would still bowl over a man like Hefner. For instance, if one were casting a film about "Hefner and his Friends," Anouk Aimée would be signed up to play Miss Bobbie Arnstein, Hefner's secretary. (Miss Arnstein, who stays up late at night *and* is promptly at her desk in the morning, seems to possess a heart of gold beneath a no-nonsense public manner; as far as I could determine, she was the only resident of The Mansion who had the Sunday airmail edition of *The New York Times* delivered to her door. "She's almost like his wife would be," an executive in the Playboy Building told me. "She runs the woman who runs the house.")

Hefner confided that before Barbara he had had "an important relationship" with a girl during the previous five years. "But this relationship to Barbara now has opened me up again emotionally. For me, the times spent alone with a girl are *the* best times.

"You know, I still have some of the Puritan heritage that I grew up with. There are gaps between what I intellectually believe in and the man I am. We're all fighting—or we should be—to become the people we ought to be. But a personal romantic relationship is the toughest; in male-female relations, I'm still in one place intellectually and another emotionally. I'm afraid I believe in a double-standard for men and women in actual situations far more than I want to admit. When I'm involved emotionally with a girl, I'm very possessive.

"Innocence still means a lot to me in a girl—you can call me old-fashioned in a way. I'm deliberately quite vulnerable in human relationships, but I'm glad to be that way because it means you always look for the best in people, girls especially. Otherwise, I might have become jaded and cynical."

One night at The Mansion, while Hefner played cards in the main room with a few of his buddies, including John Dante, one of his closest friends, who also lived at The Mansion and acted as a liaison for Hefner with the Playboy Clubs, I went swimming with Barbara in the basement pool.

"They changed my name," she told me, making a face. "Barbara Benton. Do you like it? Is it okay?" She was about to star in a movie, "How Did a Nice Girl Like You Get Into This Business?"

It was obvious that the girl was bright, excited about the possibilities of her career, eager to please, and impressed with the Hefner aura. I was struck by her self-possession when Hefner took her out "on the town" on two later evenings— an unusual practice for him, since most nights he remained inside The Mansion. One night, for example, five of us—including Hefner and Barbara, drove over to the Old Town section of Chicago, walked through a "Believe It or Not" exhibition, and then through a wax museum where the founder of *Playboy* was the first subject. When we went across the street to buy ice cream cones before going back to the car, people reacted to Hefner as if he were a Hollywood superstar, but Barbara managed to remain both calm and natural.

It was the same thing another night when I joined Hefner and Barbara at a performance of "The Man from La Mancha," and dropped in at the Pump Room of the Ambassador-East— he got instant recognition, and she stood up under the strain of intense public curiosity. Once, when we went to a large neighborhood bar where there was dancing, a bartender explained, "He comes in here because he can let go and everybody pointedly ignores him," but within a few minutes three students came over to talk. Later, Hefner and Barbara got a chance to get on the dance floor, where they performed in a fashionably mod, but not frenetic, style. Finally, we caught the last show in one of the rooms at Chicago's Playboy Club, where we were seated ringside. The comic, sparked by the presence of The Boss, put on a memorable act, but the girl singer seemed somewhat unnerved. Just before we left, a bunny came over to me and whispered, looking in Barbara's direction: "I thought I'd hate her. But she's trying so hard. I don't *dis*like her." Barbara fitted everybody's image of the-girl-next-door with her openness and unsophisticated, natural charm. I thought of something Hefner had once told me: "There's something that passes for sophistication in this society that turns me off."

One morning I joined Hefner and Barbara on a flight from Chicago to Los Angeles on his new private DC-9 jet that is painted all black except for a white bunny on its tail. Barbara was reading a self-improvement book to learn how to use new words. She came across a list of words describing phobias. "Triskaidekaphobia is the phobia about the number thirteen," Barbara told me. "And here's hydrophobia. You know, Hef has a fear of water. That's why he won't learn to swim."

I joined Barbara for lunch that included Château Lafite-Rothschild 1964, rare roast beef carved at our table, and hot croissants. She enjoys Kahlua and requested that a bottle be carried on flights. As we chatted, Barbara worked on the needlepoint that she always carries with her. She missed "Cuff," the Lhasa apso puppy given by her to Hefner, that had been left behind at The Mansion. "Cuff" was surely the most spoiled dog in the world, being coddled by Playboy bunnies at all hours of the day and night.

Aboard the private jet, we moved in luxury through the skies. Seven stewardesses—three on regular assignment, four in training—served the five passengers including myself. However, the overwhelming isolation afforded its master by the plane struck me as much as its luxury. A chauffeured limousine had delivered us to the jet's door from The Mansion, and upon arrival in Los Angeles, a shiny black Mercedes would wait outside the plane door to whisk us into the city. I thought about a crowded bus I had seen the night before on a Chicago street during rush hour. People stood, sweating, in the aisles. Bodies were jammed together. These people had taken a bus to their jobs that morning, worked hard all day, stood in line for their evening bus trip home, and then been compelled to stay yet another hour on the hot, jampacked vehicle. It seemed to me that Hefner—perhaps disguised, wearing a business suit and shades—should take such a bus trip, or a subway ride, from time to time, in order to keep in touch with ordinary people's experiences and feelings. Too many editors and publishers, as they became rich and famous, have lost that touch: one has seen them moving in a private world, dining on expense accounts in fabled restaurants while laconically pinpointing "where the action is" for armies of weary readers.

I was chatting with Jodie McRae, Hefner's forty-two-year-old black personal valet, when the plane approached Los Angeles. He left me to walk back to Hefner's bedroom door, where Barbara had joined Hefner for a nap, to alert them about the landing. "They have to get up and fasten their seat belts," I said. McRae laughed. "No," he told me. "They have bed belts they can use."

Barbara obviously meant a great deal to Hefner, but could any girl compete with the excitement Hefner felt in directing the whole Playboy complex? "You know," he told me late one night before Barbara had arrived from Los Angeles, "there are some people who even say that at heart I don't like women. It all comes out of their assumption that *Playboy* exploits women. Apparently they also theorize that a man who has been with a great many women sexually and romantically doesn't really like them; of course, what they're really doing is projecting monogamy as an ideal. For them, the Casanova syndrome is homosexual or misogynist. The fact is I have closer relations with women, on a one-to-one basis, than I do with men.

"It's true that I'm not looking for the same intellectual stimulation in women as in men. Besides, mostly I prefer younger women—maybe it's a bit of the need for an emotional island away from the storm. Not that I'm looking for the stereotyped dumb blonde—the girl I married was a school-teacher. And the last girl I went with—for more than five years —she had gone to college and was very aware, very sensitive. And Barbara can hold her end in any company. But let's face it: real intellectual drive isn't going to come from girls that age. Besides, I'm not romantically attracted to the women I find most intellectually exciting. But it's not brains that turns me off a girl; it's that emotionally castrating thing."

A few minutes later, however, he was giving me more details about the operations of the magazine, explaining that he had confidence in the people to whom he has given responsibility, and could safely stay away from The Playboy Building because of "the great personal identification they feel with me." He frowned and shook his head: "To be there, in the building—none of us would benefit from it in the long run. I'd be living my life for others rather than myself."

I was jolted back to the present as Hefner handed me a fresh drink and said earnestly, "The only thing that means anything to me is *Playboy*. Other things, if they have meaning, are extensions of the magazine. And magazines are like people, passing through stages. *Playboy* is an adult now, its youth behind it, but it still contains radical revolution within its pages."

Hefner gave me a personal tour of The Mansion in the early hours of one morning after a particularly long interview session. We lingered over details in the main room that I had not seen before, like its two secret panels, one leading to a guest chamber, the other involving a multi-level movement of the television set, a wall panel, and an oil painting. "I felt this room called for giant imagery," he said, as he gestured to the armored figure and immense paintings, the imported fireplace from Italy, and the ceiling that had been shipped from England.

"I was going to build a house," he said, "then I found this. The house is worn, used. It's not just a showplace. It's functional. Lived-in. It's probably the most famous private house in the country or the world. Shel Silverstein stayed here in a guest room that had windows on the street outside. He would overhear conversations. People were always speculating as to what mad things were going on inside."

A pair of 35 mm. movie projectors sat in an adjacent room, ready for Sunday afternoon film showings. They show up to cinemascope size when a screen comes down and covers a giant wall. (One Sunday, after a screening of *Midnight Cowboy* in the afternoon, we congregated in the room again shortly past midnight to look at one of Hefner's favorite films, *Tom Jones*.) Sometimes a special line is installed for closed-circuit TV fights; during my visit Hefner invited about a hundred people in to see the Frazier-Quarry fight in the main room. He recalled how Muhammad Ali (then known as Cassius Clay) had said once, after a fight, "I want to say hello to Hugh Hefner and all my friends in Chicago," knowing that they were at that moment watching TV at Hefner's place.

The kitchen was bigger than those in most restaurants; I looked at it, and we went downstairs to the swimming pool, with its South Seas motif, and to the underwater bar with steps copied from a Parisian cave and a fireman's pole to slide down. In the bar, too, there was a kinetic abstract painting that keeps moving, repeating itself only after two hundred and fifty hours.

"I don't need more money," Hefner told me. "To J. Paul Getty it seems important. It's not important to me whether I'm worth one hundred million or twenty million or one hundred and fifty million. What I do need is a full life and doing the things that need to be done. A full life means—well, I was in the process of becoming a recluse. I could have done it emotionally. A hardening of the emotional arteries. It's like the guy who buries himself to write a novel. It's the fact that I wasn't giving enough. Not allowing enough other people to take on the chore of the magazine. For fifteen years, at an ever increased pace, I'd been doing the same thing. I had to break the mold. The fires are still there but they have to be checked or they burn you up. Life can become routine so it is automated, passionless, destructive, repetitive. You know, money was important to me when I was poor and had to go to Carson, Pirie, Scott to explain why I couldn't pay my bills that month. But now, I don't think about it. What I really want is to extend my life several times over."

Back upstairs, Hefner showed me another special room, adapted from a *Playboy* feature story, "An Electronic Entertainment Wall." This was the world of James Bond, with video-tape machines that could transcribe up to five hours without interruption. "I've got over five hundred films on tape," Hefner said. "When I get tired of a movie, I just record over it."

In his bedroom Hefner explained that the famous circular bed had also grown out of a magazine feature. "It will move in either direction, at various speeds, and can face either video-tape equipment, a fireplace, the hi-fi, or a desk area." The bed had a built-in light control and an intercom to all rooms in the house. Alongside was a refrigerator full of Pepsi-Cola, and a nude sculpture, "Woman in a Sling Chair," had been placed in front of a fireplace. Off the dressing room, a circular stairway led downstairs to an elaborate Roman bath. Stacks of paper were all over the floor, inside the bedroom, in a long room outside it, and in his private study.

Hefner still acts personally as cartoon editor for the magazine, he explained. Cartoon finishes for future issues of *Playboy* were piled on a couch in the long room. A circular white table, surrounded by four chairs, was filled with clippings and pictures. Dummies for *The Best of Playboy* books were stacked on the floor. One table held piles of magazines—he told me that he subscribed to *Time, Newsweek, Look, Life, Horizon, Psychology Today, Mad,* and the *New Yorker.* There was an unofficial out-box: a pile of papers in front of the door of the long room. There were also three editorial in-boxes, arranged in order of priority. "If, at a certain point, I don't get to some things now, they move along anyway," he said. "Hundreds of thousands of dollars were lost because I was a bottleneck." Hefner told me that he had not yet read "The Playboy Interview" in the current issue of the magazine.

"Today I had a photo meeting with Art Paul at three-thirty and saw my son at five-thirty. He had dinner with me. Tomorrow I have two meetings. One about the clubs with Arnold Morton. It will last three or four hours. And I have an articles meeting with Spec and editorial staff people for another couple of hours."

We went into his private study: a typewriter sat by his desk. I pointed to it, as if chiding him about its recent non-use. "Oh, I'll be writing again," he said. "The Philosophy? I don't know. I stopped writing The Philosophy because there weren't enough hours in the day to do it. I was taking dexedrine and hurting my health. I enjoyed the magazine work so much I had become a cog in the machinery instead of standing on the sidelines while remaining in control. What I used to go through at deadlines was excruciating. Learning to delegate authority was like stopping smoking: you stop completely and then adjust back."

Photographs and drawings filled the wall over the desk. A satirical *Look* illustration of "Father Hefner" in clerical garb with rabbit ears. A bumper sticker: *Hugh Hefner is a Virgin, Philosophically Speaking,* that had appeared in *The Realist.* A *Time* cover on Hefner, for a story entitled "The Pursuit of Hedonism," was respectfully framed. A photo taken in London with J. Paul Getty. And a Whitney Darrow, Jr., cartoon from the *New Yorker:* the scene is a church wedding, and a bride and groom are seen standing in front of a clergyman. She wears bunny ears over veil. The caption reads, "He met her in some Chicago key club, I understand."

Over Hefner's desk was a photograph taken by Vincent J. Tajiri, *Playboy*'s picture editor: the whole photo staff is seen wearing pajamas and holding Hefner-like pipes. Nearby is an *Esquire* drawing of "Three Wise Men"—Hefner, Timothy Leary, and Billy Graham." Finally, there was a certificate that held special sentimental meaning: inscribed "to a cartoonist extraordinary," and dated September 25, 1963, it came from the National Cartoonists Society.

"I've lived a full life," Hefner said thoughtfully, "romantically and otherwise, and I don't expect to be copping out in my later years. I'm not going to start a literary magazine or sponsor opera or do things I'm not interested in as if to justify my existence. The Playboy Foundation doesn't just get into safe things, like most other foundations, but controversial areas, the same as the magazine.

"I take as much pride in who I have as enemies as who I have as friends. I've picked my side and I believe in it. This is a time of social revolution. I don't want to become the gray-haired philosopher, even if it means falling on my ass occasionally."

We moved over to the fireplace. On the mantel was a Frankenstein figure who dropped his pants, a Herb Gardner ceramic, and several Femlins—the stark white figures of nude women with black hair and black stockings ("I conceived the Femlin and LeRoy Neiman executes them"), and a large bowl of identical pipes. Above was a magazine illustration for a *Playboy* story by Jack Kerouac and a portrait of Humphrey Bogart ("I admire him as much as anyone in my lifetime").

Hefner said he was halfway through *Portnoy's Complaint*. "I keep several books on the fire at the same time." Boxes of books, unpacked, filled the center of the room.

We left the study and headed up a circular stairway to the conference room for a last drink; it was past three in the morning and my questions had evoked a mood of introspection. "I've spent evenings with eastern sophisticates, so-called," he confessed, "making a big deal out of pseudointellectuals, and getting stoned out of their minds. But I've got my own set of values and don't need to apologize or justify one part of my life by denying another.

"A lot of people assume that I'm some kind of economic entrepreneur. But at gut level no part of me—who I am as an individual—is related to my financial success. That happened as a kind of fluke, even though it grew out of what I really wanted to do.

"I'm a romantic and sentimental person, a mixture of introvert and extrovert. I have to have time alone—like I used to spend hours by myself in front of a typewriter, and I also need to meet people. F. Scott Fitzgerald said something that rings true for me—maybe it applies to lots of writers—about being in a situation and also outside it, looking at it as a third party. Like when you're on display, at a party or that kind of thing.

"There's always been a bit of show business in me. Even in grade school and high school, I was interested in acting, song writing, directing. When I was sixteen, I made a horror movie, 'Return from the Dead.' Also I did some comedies that were put on. And my best friend was a ham radio and electronics bug—he went into physics, research."

He looked out the window, and his chain of thought had shifted. "They say some people are physically night people. For me it's the romantic time, when things are happening that excite me and turn me on. It's easier to be awake and operating when other people are sleeping. And this house, I suppose it's a womb, to some extent. All of us need areas that are shelters, emotionally as well as physically. Here is a complete environment that I control. We all hope to find what is safe and secure emotionally."

I nodded agreement, but Hefner had already turned away. "You know, I realize there's some gap between The Playboy Philosophy and my own relations with girls. Intellectually you can evolve a philosophy that you believe in, but then you have to live as a human being with your own hangups. You try to bring them together. It would be very easy to turn yourself off. I'm in a position to take a great deal emotionally and give very little. But I don't. I try not to."

He came back to me, smiled, said good night, and then remembered something he'd started earlier. "You know, people in show business have a great need for public adulation and acceptance. There's a strange inconsistency in the person who, after achieving fame, then resents—or pretends to—the public attention. When I want to be alone, I'm alone. When I want to be with people, I'm out in public. And I don't resent it.

"It has to do with my image of myself—a romantic image that is a lot more important to me than the idea people have of me as a business tycoon. The romantic image is that great American dream of being accepted and admired by men, and attractive to women. To me, that's the stuff happiness is made of."

Hefner's images, of course, virtually buried Hefner the man. He felt that no writer, with the exception of Tom Wolfe, had ever done him justice in print—although, he said, he had spent as much time with press interviews as anyone in the world.

While I visited The Mansion, Gloria Steinem dropped by one afternoon to interview Hefner. She was writing a piece on *Playboy* and its master for *McCall's*. There was much speculation among The Mansion's inhabitants as to whether Miss Steinem, an avowed women's liberation militant, would be highly critical of Hefner in the piece. Hefner said afterwards that Miss Steinem told him she did not consider The Boss as antifeminist as his magazine.

Barbara Benton, who was visiting Hefner from Los Angeles, joined him and Miss Steinem for a few moments during the interview. "Gloria Steinem was very pretty," Barbara told me. "She's so *young*," Miss Steinem told Hefner after Barbara had left them. "Why did Steinem say that?" Hefner asked several of us later. "Why couldn't she have said, well, *fresh?*" "Oh, she was envious," Barbara commented, making a joke. I felt closest to Hefner when his multiple and complex images receded into the woodwork (but, I thought, he was more responsible for them than anyone else), and I found myself engaged in conversation with a fellow human.

Once I suggested to Hefner that, the next time a national magazine wanted to do a story about him, an event should be staged to meet their image requirements. Loud music should be played at peak volume in the main room of The Mansion. Naked women should run in and out of doors, screaming. The floor should be wet with flowing gin and scotch, and at least the semblance of an orgy might be staged near the swimming pool. "Then the writer could say, 'The interview exceeded even my wildest expectations,' " I explained to Hefner. He laughed.

I told him of the newspaperwoman I had met during my stay in Chicago who kept asking me, "But is he happy? How can he be *happy?*"

Hefner puffed strenuously on his pipe, then grinned. "They can't stand the fact that I'm not miserable," he said. "It would make them happier if I were miserable."

2

The Colorado Chicanos

Decolonisation never takes place unnoticed, for it influences individuals and modifies them fundamentally. It transforms spectators crushed with their inessentiality into privileged actors, with the grandiose flare of history's floodlights upon them. It brings a natural rhythm into existence, introduced by new men, and with it a new language and a new humanity. Decolonisation is the veritable creation of new men. . . .

The poster on the wall showed the strong bronze face of a man, his mouth wide open in a shout. The figure was a bold illustration for the brief, accompanying message:

Now rehearsing—The Revolutionist
An original play by Rodolfo 'Corky' Gonzalez
Needed: Workers Back Stage. See Kelly.

Frantz Fanon, *The Wretched of the Earth* (New York, Grove Press, 1966), pp. 29–30.

73

"It's Brown Power we're talking about," said the young man standing next to me in the Denver Center of the Crusade for Justice. "The blacks are ahead of us right now, sure, but we're moving fast, man. And they're nearly ten million of us Chicanos."

The Center, which had been converted from an old church building, was alive with activity. A volunteer answered the constantly ringing telephone in a no-nonsense manner, dispensing bits of information when he could, brusquely announcing that so-and-so was not there, and writing down messages in a notebook. Small children ran in and out. A dog approached everyone in turn for a pat on his head; then, tail wagging, walked outside and down the hall.

"Look at this," said the young man who had been showing me around; he handed me a form that had been sent in by a sociology student and pointed to a question that read: "What are the goals of the Hispano social movement?"

"The same old exploitation," he went on without waiting for my comment. "Some guy's going to get some big degree, be accepted as an *expert*, if we give easy answers to his simple-minded questions. And calling us Hispano—we never use 'Hispano' or 'Spanish,'" he said contemptuously. "How can they do reports when they don't know anything about us?"

I had come to Denver to learn about the movement for Chicano freedom, and because of what I had learned about Rodolfo Gonzalez, the forty-one-year-old prime mover in The Crusade for Justice. From outside, the building had seemed worn and tired, but one was struck by the bold Aztec designs painted in red on its walls, and the old school bus, parked alongside, with a new sign in giant lettering, "Chicano Power." Inside, the corridors were dark and windows looked out on a dirt lot, but everyone moved with a sense of purpose and was invariably friendly.

Gonzalez was in his office, surrounded by people—a Chicano student just returned from Mexico, two Catholic seminarians, a Mexican-American girl working as a volunteer, and a visiting couple active in the peace movement—and he simply opened up the circle to include me in the conversation. I was introduced to his wife, Gerry, who was looking for her car keys; an earnest, intense woman, she played an active role in The Crusade in addition to caring for their eight children. The photograph of one of their sons hung over Gonzalez's desk, which was filled with papers and unanswered letters. Copies of *El Gallo* ("The Fighting Cock"), the Crusade's monthly newspaper, were stacked on a nearby table, and half of one wall was covered with book shelves that gave considerable evidence of use, and on which I noted such titles as *Malcolm X Speaks, The Labyrinth of Solitude* by Octavio Paz, *The Negro Pilgrimage in America* by C. Eric Lincoln, *La Vida* by Oscar Lewis, *Mexico* by Carleton Beals, *Great River* by Paul Horgan, and *The Rich and the Super-Rich,* by Ferdinand Lundberg.

The conversation was interrupted by constant demands on Gonzalez. "Hey, Corky," someone would call out, using the nickname acquired in Gonzalez's years as a boxer, when he had been ranked as one of the world's top featherweights. "That guy from San Antonio is calling back; they want you to come down there." Gonzalez would swing his tough muscular body around to take the phone, smile at the rest of us to go on without him, handle the call briefly, and move effortlessly back into the discussion. Finally, he was drawn aside by one of his assistants, and there was an animated argument that was impossible for me to follow. "He thought I had to go somewhere to make a decision, but it's something for the neighborhood to work out," he explained. "My concept of leadership is to be an organizer and educator. Leadership isn't to control power, but to create it in people; not to control people but to teach them."

Of necessity, Gonzalez and I had most of our sessions away from the office, in time he could snatch from his many duties—sometimes in a booth at a nearby coffee shop, more often driving around town in his car or sitting in the car at a park not far from the center. Despite his frequent reference to "Anglos," he was surprisingly direct and open, his smile unforced. I was also impressed with the unaffected way in which he was involved in the community: a truck driver would wave at him from across the street, a waitress would come over in a restaurant to ask about a meeting, someone would suddenly rush out of a store to thank him for some small favor. They all admired him, it was clear, but he never tried to dominate them.

"The old political game was for the so-called leader to say, 'I have all the answers and the connections.' My concept is that we should all share the knowledge," Gonzalez told me. "All the people should be able to evaluate the system and have the confidence to create something of their own. Each person in The Crusade takes something and runs it himself. Priests, sisters, lawyers—no one can be a prima donna here. We brought lawyers up to *our* level.

"On the front line, the people have to determine what is revolution—which I define as, first, the liberation of your own mind. After you unburden yourself of the assumptions of the status quo, the hypocrisy, then you can teach others. We have to determine our own values, recognizing what's wrong with this society. Ours is a spiritual and emotional revolution, for we must develop self-confidence in our own people."

We stopped for a cup of coffee, and he folded his hands on the table with calm deliberation. His brown eyes held anger as he spoke of what he called the fatalist tendency of most Mexican-Americans, which makes them say "I'm guilty" when they are pulled into court. "It's as bad as a young Chicano saying, 'I'll go to Vietnam and kill me a commie.' This is a crazy kind of *machismo*, trying to prove he's a good guy. If I know I'm good people, why do I have to prove it to anyone?"

I knew that Gonzalez was constantly trying to build up an identification with Mexican-American history and culture, even in what at first seemed minor aspects. At the center someone had given me a study outline that he had prepared, which included the category "Food."

When I mentioned this, he smiled, but it was clear that this was a serious subject for him. "Yes," he said, "in the academic places, like the Chicano Studies curriculum at the University of Colorado, they didn't have things like that. But think of a Chicano child who goes to school with Anglo youngsters, who talk of their breakfast of bacon, eggs, and toast. He says that's what he had for breakfast, too, even though he knows it was really beans.

"But why should I deny what I am? Every Mexican has smelled *chili verde*, out of the windows of the *barrio*, as he came home from work. Food is important in our history, our culture. Take the tortilla. Where did it come from? The Spanish? No, from the Indians. When you get to know our food, you start relating to our real identity. And green chili—you won't find any better than here—it's an indigenous food.

"Music, too, is part of what we are—folk songs, chants, and dances. And the mariachi—the musical group that sings and plays for Mexicans. And do you know our dances? They tell you about our people; every section of Mexico has its own. Always, one can hear the violin and the guitar, playing ancient *corridos* and *cantos*."

I had been told Gonzalez was a poet, but had not yet read his *I am Joaquin*, an epic in which autobiographical self-discovery flowed easily into the proud stream of Chicano identity. The intensity behind the lecture he was giving me on Chicano contributions to American culture gave me some hint of how a poet could be a revolutionary.

"In the schools they don't tell the children lots of things about American history," he complained. "Like the fact that, from 1526 to around 1800, we named the streams, roads, mountains, rivers, and hills of the Southwest. The Indian, of course, was the first adobe builder, and the regional architecture is a combination of Spanish and Indian. We did the most to develop farming techniques and established certain foods.

"The black man was castrated. He couldn't make decisions for his wife, his children, or anybody. As for the Chicano, he simply withdrew. It was for self-preservation; he couldn't do anything to change things, but at least he kept his *machismo*, and his family ties."

This withdrawal of the Chicano, Gonzalez believed, had at least preserved his culture from the corruption of the Anglo system. "Let's face it," he commented, "Edward Albee says it very well; he presents *his* people as they are. But when I read his stuff, I can't identify with any of it. Those people are all screwed up. But most Americans can see themselves in his characters—they're sick. I'd worry if Chicanos were identifying with this culture."

I was impressed with the inner calm that accompanied the most militant assertion. I could not, of course, see Denver with his eyes, and wondered if he underestimated the danger of confronting the entrenched power of middle-class America. He nodded gravely at my comment. "I understand," he said slowly. "When you confront society and make clear that you will no longer exist as half a man, then they come out to destroy you. For their economy, their politics, even their sexual life, is threatened. Racism has made then paranoid; they killed Malcolm X and thought they destroyed a philosophy; they killed Martin Luther King and thought they destroyed a leader.

"We've committed our fifteen-year-olds to be men. After all, Fanon is right in a psychological sense: the slave cannot be free until he kills the oppressor. I say that you can do this intellectually, but you have to be strong enough. Hell, you're not even living unless you're involved in an action. You're not really living if you're getting callouses on your ass from watching TV or developing finger muscles by holding cans of beer."

Gonzalez drove me through the Denver slums, and his sophistication vanished as he recalled past and present terrors, both in his own experience and in that of his people. We passed a policeman. "You know," he said softly, "I was a fighter, afraid of nothing. But I was thirty before I got rid of a sense of worry, being on the defensive, whenever a policeman walked by."

He pointed to a corner drugstore. "You see there?" he asked. "Anglo truck drivers used to hang out there when I was a kid. 'All right, you dirty little Mexicans, get out of the way,' they'd yell at us. We'd fight, and then the police would come. Once I was hiding in the tall grass, and I saw the police run after Billy, a tough young Chicano, and beat him with their gun butts. They left permanent scars on his face, and his own aunt didn't know him, he was so bloody. And after they finished kicking and beating him, the police captain said, 'Throw that Mexican out here in the street and I'll drive over him with my car.' That same night, they held another guy's legs and busted both his knee caps with a club. He didn't have any hospital care and got put in the county jail for six months."

Gonzalez's life is interwoven with that of his people; to understand him, I needed to talk to those around him. Ernie Vigil, for example, was twenty-one, and in March, 1968, was the first Chicano in Denver to refuse induction into the United States armed forces. An attempt was made to induct him in March, 1969; there was a scuffle, and Vigil was charged with assaulting a Federal Marshal: maximum sentence would be three years in prison and a five-thousand-dollar fine.

"This system has always abused my people. I know how the police treated us, and how hard it was for anyone to get out of the vicious circle of poverty and frustration. The guys I grew up with never had a chance to develop what was inside them—most of them are serving time now, or out on the street drinking, or on dope. And don't tell me about education—I went to one of their schools—seventy percent black, thirty percent Mexican—and they didn't teach us a thing!"

No doubt, the police thought Vigil was a thug and his teachers had been afraid of him; I found him an intense and vulnerable young man, dressed in T-shirt and faded levis. He spoke slowly at first, and with long pauses; then suddenly his words poured out with a newfound freedom and eloquence.

"My father told me that my family had lived in New Mexico since the 1790's. Then, at school, they said I had a foreign accent, a foreign look, a foreign name. It was such an insult I didn't know how to answer them.

"I went to Manual High School here in Denver. 'You can't think, so learn to do something with your hands'—that was the administration's idea. They told us we were 'culturally deprived' and gave us assignments like, 'Write about your summer vacation.' If they'd said, 'Write about an incident between you and a cop,' we'd have come up with some pretty fantastic stuff.

"But the Chicanos have always resisted what has been happening to them. Do you remember the *Pachuco?*" I recalled vaguely how in the early 1940's the mass media had coopted a Hollywood version Mexican-American stocktype, complete with long flashy coat, baggy pants, and a long, looped gold keychain. "It was simply rebellion," Vigil said, "on the part of young guys, who weren't political in those days, but wanted to be themselves. Their dress and hairstyles were a way of thumbing their noses at society—I'm going to be something you don't want to look at.

"We've learned from the blacks: you don't get anywhere suffering silently and in dignity. You've got to let them know you don't like it, and if that means violence, that's the way it has to be. In this society, no one listens to words anyway. The only things the system understands are force and money. But it's different now. It used to be, 'You either give me all or nothing.' Now, it's 'I'm going to have it all. And if I don't get it, we're *both* going to pay.'

"You know, when I was growing up, I was trying to make money to apply for college. I did this by selling grass. I was identifying with what a hood in the street knows: this society places a value on money, especially fast money. You can't make it downtown, or go to work for your father's firm, but you can do a bit of hustling on a lot of side streets.

"Later, I went to college for about two years in Vermont, and began to find out some of the things that had been kept from my people. If they'd gotten the education the kids there had, it would have made them radical. The place was antiwar, and we even got an understanding of Marxism."

The education Vigil received, however, only deepened the problem of identity. "For years the Chicano has listened to the dialogue between black and white, wondering where he belonged. Our culture is so different from both; right now, black is just a mirror of what the white has done to it. As for middle-class Chicanos, they're almost as badly off; a Chicano hood on the west side here has more identity than a guy with a briefcase who has sold his soul. At least the hood isn't alienated from himself, or a robot. And he's got a whole code of the way you do things—like not blowing your cool. The less you expose yourself to this society, the less liable you are to be wounded.

"There are two main reactions to Chicanos from Anglos. First, 'They're communists,' or 'Why don't you go back to where you came from?' Second, the liberal, polite way of co-opting you with sensitivity programs and job training. Quite a few of our people are being coopted. They say, 'Before you destroy this system, you have to infiltrate it, and try to change it.' "

Vigil told me he had been moved by James Baldwin's novel, *Another Country*. "Not that Baldwin is politically aware, but I like the way he describes what it is to be black—the whole scene. A guy pissing in an alley, and the steam rising from his piss. I'd like to write about a gang, the dignity and tragedy of what it means to be Chicano and to have grown up on the streets."

I asked him about other Chicano leaders.

"Cesar Chavez is always appealing for support and sympathy," he complained. "I don't dig that sympathy thing. I don't care whether you like me or hate me—just know me. Reies Tijerina's issue is good—he's demanding the return of our land, and that's something our people relate to. Chavez is trying to be inoffensive because he has to raise more money.

"I'm no leader, and I wouldn't be one. It means a lot of responsibility, and this society is so corrupt, sincerity comes hard. The government hires a Chicano with a briefcase and says, 'You're a leader.' They say Corky is 'self-appointed'— which is bullshit. The people in this organization chose Corky, and he deserves it by his character. Hell, he could go out and in two weeks have a big business or consultant job."

In a back copy of *El Gallo*, I had come across the words, "our ancient Indian universe." What did they mean to Ernie Vigil?

A faraway look came over him. "At one time, there was a people at peace with itself," he said reflectively. "Then white European invaders came, and a whole orientation was lost. There was nothing you could turn to; it was as if your gods had deserted you. The Spaniards were cruel to the Indians, but for the Puritans and Quakers in the United States, Chicanos didn't even exist.

"I grew up with a junkyard in back of us, a packing house at one corner, a lumber yard at the other. The block was full of empty lots and rundown houses. It was hopeless, but people like Corky gave me a whole new way to look at things instead of just getting a job to take care of myself; they helped me understand *La Raza*—that I must remain with my people."

In building the movement, Gonzalez puts primary emphasis on the participation of the young, feeding their intensity, providing it with nutrition and discipline. "The young are the only ones who will move," he asserted. "But for us it is necessary to emphasize the family culture, with no generation gaps. Chicanos are the only group in the country where the older people are supporting the young. And don't forget: between fifty and sixty percent of the Chicano population is under twenty-five. We're developing leadership: one percent of the population moves the rest."

In pursuit of this end, in March, 1969, The Crusade for Justice had been host to the first National Chicano Youth Conference attended by almost fifteen hundred young people representing more than a hundred organizations. Participants had come, not only from all over the Southwest, but from Alaska, Illinois, Michigan, and New Jersey. One student activist to whom I spoke was particularly impressed by the fact that two busloads of Puerto Ricans had come all the way from New York. "The Puerto Ricans are brown brothers," he said proudly. "I think they *are* Chicanos. But sometimes I wonder a little—is asking Puerto Ricans to relate to Mexico like Anglos forcing John Wayne on us?"

El Gallo's report on the meeting caught the sense of nationalistic celebration: "Conference is a poor word to describe these five days. It was in reality a fiesta. Days of celebrating what sings in the blood of a people who, colonized into believing they are ugly, discover the truth of the secret whisperings of bronze beauty nourished and guarded during years of occupation and intimidation—*we are beautiful.*"

An atmosphere of joyful brotherhood won out over the difficulties of organization, even though most of The Crusade for Justice staff had been in jail the week before, after a demonstration at West High School protesting alleged racial insults leveled at Chicano students by an Anglo teacher.

"Somehow, the conference structured itself," Gonzalez laughed. "There were art groups, some short plays, poetry readings, and workshops on all our problems. There was a women's liberation caucus—as you know, it is a sharp departure from our past for women to have a leadership role with us. The girls stayed in homes in the neighborhood, the boys lived in makeshift dorms at The Center. There were three gangs from Chicago, including the Young Lords; they got to fighting, but we got their leaders together, and explained brotherhood. Believe it or not, by the time they left, they were really living it."

During the conference, I learned, the eldest daughter of

Corky and Gerry Gonzalez was married in a ceremony at The Crusade for Justice; the report in *El Gallo* speaks for itself:

> *Two young people decided that their marriage would be a symbol of the new Movement and a unifying force for La Raza.*
>
> *Corky Gonzalez drew blood of the new bride and groom, which was crossed, and so they were married. A loyal partisan priest blessed the rites in the name of the God of Che, the God of Reies Tijerina, and the God of Cesar Chavez.*
>
> *The "amen" was soulfully stirring:*
> *"Chicano," said the priest.*
> *"Power," repeated the people.*
> *"Viva la Causa!" enjoined Corky.*
> *"Viva," was the support of the audience.*
> *"Viva," applauded everyone.*
>
> *And the Chicano applause continued for almost five minutes, first with the manifestation of unity in the hands, and then with a solidarity of stamping with the feet, accompanied by the fervent yelling characteristic of joy.*
>
> *Meanwhile everyone on the stage embraced and kissed each other. The band was playing a stirring revolutionary polka. In this way is defiance spread through the blockaded land of Aztlán—defiance and pride and the will for survival. Viva Aztlán!*

Aztlán is a geographical reference to the former northern territories of Mexico, stretching from southern California as far as Nebraska. It is also a rallying cry for liberation and national control of institutions. The youth conference issued "The Spiritual Plan of Aztlán," which was described as "a call to unity as a nation of people." Gonzalez contributed significantly to the writing of the document, but the preamble was composed by a group of poets and artists across the country. Indeed, everything I heard about the conference suggested that, in accordance with Gonzalez's theory of leadership, it was designed to develop the young people's capacities for making decisions and taking complete charge of local situations. "We don't know how far we're going," Gonzalez told me. "What we're doing today, the younger guys may take much further."

Many of the key people at The Crusade are young, and their commitment is total. Antonio, for example, in his early twenties, his hair in something very close to an Afro cut, spoke with barely controlled rage about what he had seen and the history of his people.

"The oppressors were once very few, and my forefathers could have exterminated them all," he reminded me. "But they waited, and suddenly my forefathers had chains on their necks and knees. My mothers were white men's servants and lovers. My land, I no longer owned, although I worked it. My people starved, while the white man took the profits. I say just one thing: he's got to go.

"If we are to have a chance to be free, this system must be exterminated. Let's be honest: I don't really believe in white friends. They talk sweet, but do they ever do anything—and I'm not interested in their money: we need results."

Antonio spoke freely about his estrangement from his own family.

"I'm not recognized by them. They wanted me to stay in their house and go on to study for a Ph.D. They believe in money, but money can't bring happiness. My life doesn't belong to me; I have to work for my people and destroy the oppressor.

"I went to college for three and a half years—got good grades and everything—but I wasn't learning a damned thing. The only good thing I did was organize. Then, about a year ago, I just couldn't take it any longer. Hell, those institutions aren't going to work for us until we change the whole system."

His view of the future was equally uncompromising. "Revolution is bound to come soon. All the professional politician wants is individual power. People will have to choose what side they're on; whoever goes with the minority must be ready to die. We know we'll be the first persons down, but that doesn't mean a thing. Because, finally, success will be ours —or at least for our kids."

Art Cordova, twenty-one, and just reclassified 1A, is another Chicano youth who is deeply involved with The Crusade for Justice. "You've got to understand," he said urgently, "how a Mexican kid looks at white power—it's pretty big and frightening. He feels stupid and lazy—that's the role he's been assigned—and when he gets big, he doesn't feel good about himself.

"Corky makes people damned proud of who they are, teaching them about their culture and history, how Anglo society destroyed what the Mexican had created, how the white power structure works, and how they can fight back. The old won't change, but the young are starting to think more radically. The question is: how to destroy the present economic and political system and replace it with something more responsive to the people.

"Some speak of nonviolent revolution, but this would probably only be able to come about through separation— brown control of as much as possible, both our economy and politics. But are the people who are manipulating it now going to turn it over to us peacefully? If not, how can we take it away from them nonviolently?

"Some black people are being funded now to begin capitalism in their own communities—they're getting bought in the process. Capitalism is exploitative, regardless of black or white or brown. It's not an accident that the Mexican-American has received the least education in the Southwest."

Cordova pointed to a picture of Che Guevara on a book cover. "What he did for Cuba was unbelievable; violent revolution worked there. Here it would be begun in the ghettos and *barrios*, with people burning and destroying. But whether or not we have to have a violent revolution depends on the white power structure. It could relax its grip on people—if they were willing to do that. Or they could feel so threatened that suppression would get worse, until revolution exploded."

As with Antonio, there was a painful break with his own family. "I was raised in a middle-class neighborhood and robbed of my own identity. Until I got into The Crusade, I didn't know who I was. Now, at an Anglo party, I really feel alienated; those people make me sick, especially the white missionaries who say, 'Don't cut yourself off from me because I can do a lot for you.' It's like the old *patrone*, who had economic power, talking to the peon.

"One of my relatives says, 'I made it by hard work; the Mexican doesn't work.' He was brainwashed. I try to change his mind, but it's hopeless; everyone else in the family thinks of themselves as Spanish—I'm the only Mexican. They hate the word 'Chicano'—I was brought up thinking I was Spanish. In fact, I have some Indian blood, and some of my ancestors came from Mexico.

"I'm going to Mexico this weekend for the first time since I was a kid. You see, everything, the whole spirit of what we have and are, comes from there; even the little Spanish I learned in school isn't what is spoken in Mexico. Nationalistically, Mexico has to mean more to me than the United States."

Nevertheless, Cordova spoke of the dangers of ethnocentrism; he was trying to reconcile his identification with *La Raza* with his recollection of Che's injunction that a revolutionary has to live in terms of worldwide revolution. "Of course I'm ready to share whatever *La Raza* means with other people—white, black, yellow, whatever. But *La Raza* means Aztlán; right now I can't feel as close to the Third World as to Mexico.

"But Che—you know, he is like one of us; he is our hero." Cordova spoke with as much delivery as if he were referring to his fiancée. "He was fantastically brilliant; he really knew what was happening in the world, and what in hell the United States was up to. Nixon didn't have to send Rockefeller to Latin America to find out what it was all about; he could have read Che, and really learned something."

I asked him about his own future. "Well, you know I've just been made 1A, so I could be in prison soon. If I'm not in prison, I'll be working in the revolution, whatever way I can. I still ask myself, 'Am I willing to be a revolutionary?' Because anyone who says yes to that has to realize that his life may be up at any time."

Eloy Espinoza, thirty-eight, who is in charge of security at The Crusade for Justice, wore a brown beret with a red star, imitating Guevara. A self-educated man, he had read widely about Chicano history and culture and tried to instill young people at the center with a down-to-earth understanding of *La Raza*. "Don't go to jail for stealing a hubcap or armed robbery or stealing from a brother—if you have to be jailed, let it be for an act of revolution: this is what I tell the younger brothers," he told me. "And when you see a brother in the neighborhood being brutalized by the police, and you try to break it up so that the brother isn't hurt any more, then, if you're arrested, it's also for an act of revolution. And if the man—the pig—comes into a house by breaking down the door, and you try to stop him, that's an act of revolution."

Espinoza was harsh in his judgment on property owners in the community and insisted that the majority of them were Jewish. "They have to be driven out," he exclaimed, "so that our people can control their own lives. If a businessman is draining money from the people and taking it back to the suburbs where he lives, and not doing anything for the area where he makes his money, he should be removed. If a person in the neighborhood has no food in the house and no means of getting it, or needs legal help, a businessman should donate a percentage of his profits to help these community needs. I'm not talking just about Chicanos, but all the poor. If the men exploiting the poor in the community don't leave voluntarily, we'll drive them out, by whatever means."

I asked him to describe his functions as security officer for The Crusade.

"I'm trying to build up a force to patrol our own communities. We'll avoid violence, as much as possible, but if we have to use force, we will. Let's say I get a phone call from someone who says two or three police cars are at his house, and someone is pounding on his door. I'll go over to see what legal procedures are involved and see that no brutality is practiced against anyone who may be arrested. I'll make sure that they let him go to the police car on his own and that there are witnesses. If he has no bruises coming out of the house, he'd better not have any when he comes out of jail.

"I believe in legal process, but it's not holding up here in Denver. Our brothers are picked up and brutalized. The police come into our community after curfew, take kids to juvenile hall, and hold them there. There's always double standards: a Chicano kid is taken in and held for a criminal charge; an Anglo kid, picked up for the same thing, has his parents called, and there is no criminal record. I've tried talking to The Establishment diplomatically; nothing has been accomplished —something more drastic is needed."

Espinoza had been radicalized by his experience of injustice as a Chicano teenager and had been further discouraged by his period in the army. Discrimination, he was convinced, had prevented him from being promoted during his service in Germany. Then, at the discharge center, he had been told it would be easier to get a better job, but he ended up in the same place as before—as a truck driver and radio operator.

His reading of history had given him a sense of purpose: "It tells you who you are. After all, we have been oppressed for over two hundred years. If we cannot be free within this country, we should liberate ourselves and become a separate nation. This is why we have named this part of the country Aztlán again.

"When the Indians migrated here from across the Bering

Strait, they went down the coast and up the gulf, and into the southern part of this country, and Central and South America. There were the Mayans, the Incas (who produced the most perfect calendar), and the Aztecs, whose civilization was the most advanced of all—because of their agricultural system, their architecture, the traditions they held among themselves, their scientific developments, and their brotherhood.

"Indians have been told they were cruel, but this was their way of worshipping God. Besides, who knows what God looked like? He could have been Chinese or an Indian; for years I was worshipping a blond man with blue eyes. But I believe there was a Christ, and that he died for the same thing we're fighting for."

Emilio Dominguez, forty-seven, is vice-chairman of The Crusade for Justice, and has been with it since its inception in 1966. He had a large black beard, wore his long hair in a *chongo*—"the way the Indians wear hair," he explained, giving it the appearance of being tied in the back—and seemed to be a man of infinite patience and inexhaustible energy. At The Center his nickname was Zapata. "I consider myself as a people's counselor," he said.

Dominguez's personal history had convinced him that America's grand rhetoric about equal opportunity was completely hollow. "I was left out even as a child," he explained, "and only had a fourth-grade education when I went into the service at sixteen—I lied, I told them I was seventeen. I'm a *campesino*, born and raised in the migrant labor camps, moving around with my family, working in the fields.

"When I went into the service, I thought I'd have an opportunity to come back as somebody and help my family. It was an empty dream—six years in the infantry and when I came back, I couldn't even get a job.

"But I could go to school with my GI benefits—elementary school, high school, and college, all in six years. There was a kind of opportunity school in Oakland, California; I had gone there to play baseball—they were trying to organize a team, but it didn't work out. I went to school not so much to learn as to be able to make a living, and worked part of the time, of course. I graduated from the University of California in Berkeley in 1952, majoring in politics.

"My biggest mistake was learning how to read English. I couldn't master Spanish. My dad said I was an American of Spanish descent—it was only later that I learned about the annihilation of the Indian. If I say I'm Spanish, I'm denying my mother, who is very much Indian; she was raised with the Taos Indians in New Mexico."

I asked Dominguez about the beginnings of The Crusade for Justice.

"Our goal was to unite the people. We started April 29, 1966. I can't forget the date because that was the night I said it doesn't matter what happens—if we get that poor, we'll all eat rock soap. After that, everybody called me rock soap. I remember asking myself, what's going to happen? I didn't know about security except on the basis we'd been taught. Now I realize it's easier knowing there is no security than imagining something that doesn't exist.

"When Corky headed the Neighborhood Youth Corps, I went with him as an assistant; when he was fired, I went too. There were men from Washington there and they kept me for an hour, asking me to stay; I told them to go to hell —I couldn't see any man filling Corky's shoes. I said that the man who did the job was gone, and I was going with him. Later, there was a Chicano boycott of the *Rocky Mountain News* because of their criticism of Corky's work.

"The first Crusade headquarters was at Twentieth and Larimer, where Corky once had a bond office. We never had formal membership; people belong at their own discretion. There are no dues. We put out a biweekly paper, filled with things people would want to ask but couldn't before, because there was no forum.

"Some time later, my wife and I decided to go to Mexico

with our three children, to study the revolution. Emiliano Zapata was our ideal. We only had about one hundred and twenty dollars altogether. We just took enough clothes and got a ride to Juarez, then a train to Mexico City—I look so much like a Mexican they didn't even ask for my papers.

"My wife and I went to the university for three months, and the children went to parochial school. Most of the time we just sat around, rapping with people, learning a lot that way. Once, however, we went to a cowboy picture that was playing just around the corner. It was a big disappointment to see Mexican kids being brainwashed: the cavalry was routing the Indians, and they were cheering! Our kids said, 'What's wrong with them? Don't they know they're Indians, too?'

"Then we moved to a village thirty miles southwest of Mexico City—we wanted to get away from American tourists— it was close enough to come back and use the city libraries. People out there didn't accept us right away; it was more than a month before they realized we were the same people as they were, that we talked and laughed and smiled the same way.

"We had to carry our water from across the street, and there was an outside toilet, but I put electricity in the house. A friend had rabbits, and they were my lawnmower. You know, I hated to come back. But I knew that if I didn't, I was running away from my people's problems. Besides, it was the spring of sixty-eight and the Poor People's Campaign was beginning and I thought it couldn't go on without me."

Talking with Dominguez always led back to the everyday conditions still faced by Chicanos in Denver. "It's a disgrace that there's still hunger here," he said. "Today alone I fed three families—eighteen people—and I'll probably have to take care of them again tomorrow. But it isn't just hunger from the stomach; it's mental, spiritual. People want to learn and be free, and they can't with this situation.

"I had to be in court this morning for two hours because it was a sixty-seven-year-old Chicano man—he couldn't speak English—who had a fight with a thirty-five-year-old Anglo.

The Chicano was going to get fourteen years. What saved him was that I was interpreting in English what he *wasn't* saying in Spanish—hell, he wanted to tell the court he was proud to have used a short penknife in self-defense. He had acted like a man, and he would take their lousy fourteen years —damn fool; how do you get someone like him to realize the law isn't interested in how proud you are?

"On the way back, I stopped to see a lady whose sixteen-year-old daughter had taken off last night. She was afraid to have the police know, because they'd put the girl in juvenile hall. She wasn't sure whether the girl had just left or been taken away, but she'd rather take a chance on not seeing her than get mixed up with the police.

"We no longer depend on the police for what we used to call protection; we'd rather suffer the consequences. I get calls all night. I got one call at three A.M.—a lady who said her husband was threatening her with a knife. I woke my wife up and told her, 'If I go there, I might get killed. If I call the police, I'll have to get the guy out of jail tomorrow.' Anyway, I got up at six and went to the address; I wasn't sure what I'd find. They were both stretched out, drunk. It made me ask all over again: Why can't we trust the police? Because they were drunk, the police would have beat them up. Then we'd have to get them out of the hospital or out on bail. It's that bad.

"Not long back two young guys—one Mexican, one black —were shot, right on the street, by the police. We had a march, without a permit; we started out separately and were to meet at the city jail at two P.M.; there were six hundred Mexicans and three hundred blacks. We told them it was the last time we come there peaceably.

"There've been quite a few confrontations. The carnation growers didn't want to accept a union as bargaining agent. There were several incidents, and one of Corky's daughters was run over by a car and hospitalized. A guard was injured. A whole posse of white racists waited for us on horseback; they had big sticks and wanted to do us in."

It was not simply coincidence that the biggest confrontation to date between The Crusade for Justice and The Establishment took place at Denver's West High School in March, 1969. When Gonzalez drove me by the school in his car, he said dryly, "Three and a half months ago a lot of Chicanos here didn't know who they were. Now they know."

Another young Chicano with whom I talked at Crusade headquarters explained that the situation at the school developed after one white teacher had been particularly insulting to Chicano students. "Of course, these things have been going on for years in many different schools," he said. "For a long time we tried to keep our people calm and avoid a fight. So it was easy to bring them together on the issue; they all could remember so many wrongs. We went to the school to confront the principal but he called the police rather than meet with us.

"There were about a thousand of us, mostly students, and about a hundred concerned parents. They used helicopters to spray gas on the people; then later they said it was a mistake. The gas hit mothers and babies. That only meant that more people came out the second day. Again the police attacked the people, and this time the people fought back. There was brick and bottle throwing, injuries and arrest; some charges are still pending.

"The second night the people packed Crusade headquarters, then marched through City Hall and on to the jail. Fifty-seven of our people were in jail, including Corky. He told them he wouldn't come out until all our people were out. Then, he still wouldn't come out until a black reporter for a Denver paper was released."

For Gonzalez, the strategy used with the school board dovetailed with the constructive possibilities of confrontation. As he explained, "Action politicizes people into what revolution is about. As Castro and Guevara showed, decisions can be made on the front, not just by a few people in big city office buildings. I made the school board realize there were no negotiations possible with us. 'You made *your* decision; *we'll* answer

it,' I told them. 'You'll be responsible for any actions or violence that comes out of it.' "

The logic of the Chicano movement requires that the
school be made responsive to community needs, and the development of its own identity. In this regard, as the confrontation at West High School demonstrated, the younger students are really ahead of their elders at the universities. Manuel
Lopez, twenty-six, and a senior at the Denver center of the
University of Colorado, agreed. "We college students don't
have the understanding and political awareness to organize the
people. Some youths in The Crusade are going into the *barrios*
and pulling our high-school kids together; on a heart level,
I can relate to them, but not in language. What happened at
West was almost a scream: 'Get off my back.' The alienation
is already there; the political awareness will come next."

Lopez had founded the United Mexican-American Students (UMAS) on the Denver campus, but at the beginning
he told me, he was very pessimistic about what could be accomplished by his group. "Now," he said cautiously, "I see
a ray of hope. We'd been playing the gringo's game, wheeling
and dealing for a power we didn't have, but we're finished with
that approach."

Lopez and I went out for supper at a restaurant not far
from the center, a place where his wife, Lorraine, worked as
a waitress. He introduced me to her with obvious pride, and
they chatted for a moment in Spanish. When she left, he told
me that she was learning to read English and intended to complete her high-school education.

I asked Manuel why he remained within the university,
since he criticized it so bitterly.

"It's still one of the few institutions that has a capacity for
change," he answered. "Besides, it's an integral part of the
system; if you knocked it out, the whole system would col-
lapse. That's a good reason for getting Chicanos in.

"Besides, without the tools that the university provides,
you don't have the range of choices to accept or reject—you're

poor because you have no choice; you're a dropout because you never had a choice. I can't make such a choice for other people.

"My obligation is to change the university so that Chicanos don't come out of it as robots, but have the strength and expertise to come back to their communities and help. What's discouraging is to see how many of our students have accepted the Protestant ethic; a lot of them see Corky through Anglo eyes as simply a loudmouthed troublemaker. In their hearts, they're still white. But some of them are beginning to confront realities they had avoided before; I'd say we've radicalized a hard core of, say, fifteen. Of course, they're still tied to the system, as I am, economically."

UMAS had presented the university with a "Proposal for a Chicano Studies Program," recommending the establishment of a separate college as the most suitable vehicle for its implementation. "Spanish departments are controlled by 'Spaniards,'" Manuel explained, "who have no idea of what we're talking about. In our proposal we pointed out that if existing university departments haven't been able to develop multiethnic approaches to history, art, and literature in all these years, they're not going to do it now. They're not suddenly going to get enthusiastic about something they always rejected or considered academically irrelevant."

The theme of Chicano education ran like a steel thread through almost all my talks with Gonzalez. He referred to the influence of Ricardo Flores Magon, a journalist who died in Leavenworth Prison. "He knew that the schools did not teach the historical achievements and cultural characteristics of the Chicano, but acted merely as another link in the dehumanizing chain of Anglo institutions. Magon did what Debray has done now, helping to set the stage for a genuine popular movement. He taught the people that they have to control their own institutions. He spread his ideas by the word—repeating them over and over. At The Crusade we plant the seed in our young children. The people learn to say that the school system is ours and does not belong to the school board. And Magon also reminded us of the importance of poetry, something we encourage at the center—there is no revolution without a poet. There could have been no Castro without a José Marti; now Cuba has Carlos Guillen and other good poets."

I told Gonzalez that much of the thinking in the "Proposal for a Chicano Studies Program," which Manuel Lopez had shown me, reminded me of the demands for Black Studies Programs at other universities. "Yes," he agreed, "but we have maintained at least a semblance of our culture. It's important that we have retained our own names—they haven't been changed as the black men's names have been. The blacks talk about Africa, but the link has been broken; our heritage affirms our relationship with the Latin American *mestizo* who is truly our brother. Look at Ruben Dario, the poet, who came out of northern Mexico—he mentions all the great Indian leaders; it's amazing how many of our ideas for social changes he was already expressing."

Gonzalez was encouraged by his belief that many whites of the younger generation were receptive to his ideas and were beginning to learn the truth about Chicanos. "They're ashamed of the hypocrisy of their parents. They know that the Chicano predates Plymouth Rock by twenty thousand years on one side of his heritage, and that in this part of the country we predate the Anglo by three hundred years. But there are still problems, because there is nothing contemporary about us in print for serious people to learn from; we haven't had access to publication. Even Oscar Lewis—he's a tremendous writer—but he just discusses one family in Mexico, and he stereotypes all of us."

Lopez and the other UMAS members I had talked to had all emphasized the importance of gaining recognition for Chicano Spanish, which they considered as much an American dialect as Boston, middle-western, or southern variants of American English. Gonzalez nodded vigorous agreement as they explained that the Chicano possesses a wealth of historical information in his own language, but that his children are subjected to embarrassment and even punishment when they enter schools where only standard Spanish is spoken. They directed my attention to specific paragraphs of their "Proposal for a Chicano Studies Program," insisting on familiarity with Spanish literature, Indian treatises, and Mexican literature, "since the Chicano is a mixture of the Spanish and Indian." Literature should be analyzed in the light of specific cultural traits— "stoicism, individualism, *machismo*, spiritualism, anticlericalism, Spanish humor, and the concept of honor to name only a few." Gonzalez and the UMAS members were concerned about getting key books needed for such courses translated immediately into English, since the courses would be taught in English.

Emilio Dominguez seemed to sum it up for all of them. "Our kids are dropping out of school because they can't identify anymore with George Washington and the blond image. They're really being pushed out; in order to have any interest, they need to be able to identify. Look, everybody has been losing by half-truths, including the Anglo. What's so bad about telling the truth about *our* contributions? Why can't the white Anglo-Saxons learn from us as well?"

The Chicano Studies Program was still largely theoretical for me; the failure of current education to prepare the Chicano to deal with the dominant American society was concretized, however, by Ricardo Romero, thirty-two, another active member of The Crusade.

"When I started school, I couldn't speak English—it took me almost two years to learn. So when I was in the fourth grade, I was about the equivalent of a second grader. When I was in the sixth grade, I quit school.

"At school, we took *tortillas* and *burritos* for lunch; all the Anglo kids had sandwiches. We would hide to eat, for we were ashamed to eat this food in front of them. In class I always felt dumber than the other kids. To go through that system and identify as a Mexican is to identify as a failure. For success is blond hair and blue eyes and a dollar sign. We didn't exist in their textbooks, which were completely racist.

"Of course, there was a lot of segregation in Brighton, where I grew up. Movies were open for Mexicans on Tuesday and Thursday nights. The Catholic church had Mexican sections, separating us from the other people who worshipped there."

The school's irrelevance was only highlighted by the realities of Romero's childhood.

"There were twelve in my family," he said. "The only way we could survive was by the whole family working—my sisters were better workers than a lot of men. My father used to show us the beet fields he had contracted for—we were migrant farm workers—they would look like there was no end, beets as far as the eye could see. I did this from when I was eight 'till when I was eleven. I used to look at my mother in the rows of beets and dream that some day she wouldn't have to work like an animal.

"Then I worked as a busboy for a year and a half. At fourteen I was working in a foundry, but they laid me off when they found out my age. After that, I had different factory jobs. I was married when I was seventeen. All that time I thought of myself as a Spanish-American because that's what my father said we were.

"Then I began to read and study, and I realized we were a *mestizo* people. Our Indian blood is what purifies us. My mother is an Apache; our Indian blood relates us to the earth. As long as you don't abuse the earth, you can get anything from it. My parents had to relate to the earth; we supplied ourselves with vegetation growing along the river beds. The problem of the white man today is that he has abused the earth. Because I was raised in a rural area, I didn't have my language and culture completely destroyed, as it would have been in the city."

Romero had given up on conventional politics and

believed that the destruction of the Indian in the United States was a darker page of history than the Nazi extermination of the Jews. "I've committed my life to the Chicano movement," he said darkly, "and the only thing we have to look forward to is a bullet in the head or a long prison sentence. But we're teaching our children what it's all about, and they'll have to deal with them. And once we make a cultural tie with our fatherland—this is already happening; there is revolution brewing in almost every Latin American country—then we are no longer a minority; we become the majority."

I had expected that Catholicism would be a focal point of Chicano identity, and was unprepared for the bitterness directed against the institutional church. "I was baptized a Catholic when I was a baby," Gonzalez explained. "But my mother was a Presbyterian. When I was young, I went to church by myself. My father, coming out of the Mexican revolution, was very anticlerical; he said God was in our home.

"I was quite close to Catholicism when I was about sixteen. Then, as I got involved with social action, I saw there was no support from politicians or from my own church. I still have hopes of changing the Church, however, and my children go to Catholic schools because there we always know where they are, and the education is better than in the public school.

"For me, God is like a mother who creates—women are the only real creators; men are just artificial creators, like poets and playwrights. Something created us. We should accept the teaching not only of Jesus, but of all great men who have taught brotherhood. But I'm not a mystic; I don't believe that God is going to perform miracles to solve our problems. There have been no miracles to alleviate the pain of the poor —in Africa, Latin America, or here. When the poor develop faith in themselves to change inequities, then the Church will be theirs. But now, the Church is simply part of the whole money system; it deals in dollars, not human beings. Why are all the new churches built in the suburbs?"

The other men with whom I spoke at the center were even more critical of the failure of the Church to help the Chicano.

"My mom is Catholic," Ernie Vigil told me. "It's a cultural thing; it gives you a place, if not in the white man's world, at least in the world of God. They get all dressed up in their best clothes for church, as if God gave a damn what they wore. One of my best friends—he got killed last year in Vietnam—was an altar boy; out behind the church we used to find trash cans filled with empty wine and beer bottles—that was our Irish pastor.

"Most young people won't go to church now. They're mostly agnostics. They feel Christ died two thousand years ago; what's it got to do with now? I've yet to meet a Chicano who said, 'Yeah, I met Christ the other day, and he helped me out in court.' "

One Sunday morning I saw Chicano pickets—most of them young men—marching outside the Roman Catholic Cathedral, carrying signs that startled the predominantly middle-class whites who were arriving to attend Mass. Fathers pulled their families together defensively as they rushed past shouting pickets to the stained-glass security of the church. "We're protesting," Art Cordova explained, "because the Church refused to give one hundred thousand dollars for the United Mexican-American Student scholarship fund. We expected something more, after all the money that Chicanos have for years paid into bingo games and all the building fund drives that depended on Mexican-American loyalty to the Church."

Emilio Dominguez continued the hard note of criticism. "The Church is to blame for our lack of mobility; we've been a captive audience.

"Why wasn't the church a home away from home for us, in terms of education and recreation? We haven't been accepted in the church as people—it's an Irish domain. I don't know of one Chicano bishop."

"And when they decided they wanted a Spanish-speaking priest," Gonzalez added, "where did they go? All the way to Spain—how do they expect a Franco-trained priest is going to relate to Chicanos in the Southwest?"

"Christ was just as much a revolutionary as we are," insisted Eloy Espinoza. "He tried to tell the people the truth, and he died for it. We feel we have to sacrifice ourselves so that our people can finally have justice and freedom."

Art was another area of primary concern at The Crusade, both as an element of popular education and an invitation to individual liberation. Manuel Martinez, twenty-one, who lived with his wife, Sally, and their baby in the basement of The Crusade headquarters, was a good example of the latter possibility.

"I was raised in the black ghettos of Denver," he told me. "One of twelve children. My parents came here from New Mexico. I started stealing when I was nine or ten; I'd been to juvenile hall eleven times by the time I was thirteen. I was really messed up; in the next couple of years I was sent three times to the industrial school for boys.

"I was kicked out of school in the ninth grade; we used to spend our lunch money on wine. Then I was on the streets and got busted for burglary.

"The way I started to draw was in the reformatory, in a tiny room with a toilet, a cot, and a sink. They handed you your food. I was there two weeks. When they let us out in the day room, I used to pick up paper towels and matchsticks so that I could do charcoal drawings back in my cell.

"One time I had a bad earache. I told the nurse, and she gave me some scrap paper—backs of mimeograph paper—and a pencil; she had to sneak them to me. I did drawings of the room, the bed, my hands. She gave me a picture of her husband, and I did a sketch of it and she liked it. After that, I got allowed in the print shop and started to become known there as an artist. This gave me confidence, and they let me do a mural in the recreation room. Then I became a trustee and could go all over the place, doing drawings. I got put into an art class, and we had a contest with other institutions—I can still show you the prizes: a first in watercolor and painting, a second in pencil drawing.

"When I got out, I entered the tenth grade, and got into some art classes—one in sculpture, another in painting and drawing—and won some awards. But I started messing up with my old friends and got busted again for burglarizing a house. At the reformatory they weren't very surprised to see me back; they knew that, except for my art, I was still messed up.

"I got out again and was able to go into the eleventh grade. That year I was dealing weed; it was the only way I had friends. The black cats, who were older and bought weed from me, would always defend me. I was in reformatory another time, but the last time I got busted, for three joints of marijuana, I beat the case because of illegal search.

"The guy who really helped me was Bill, a painter-poet who started an apprentice program mainly for blacks and Chicanos. He'd go to the high schools in the ghettos and would ask art teachers for recommendations. The teachers at my school—one was black, the other was Anglo—recommended me. This painter went to my house and asked my mother, 'Where can I find Manuel?' She told him I had been in jail for two weeks, so he went to the jail and said he'd try to get me out and I could live with him and some of his other apprentices. He sold his Volkswagen and Corky threw in one hundred and fifty dollars as my bond.

"I lived with Bill for about three years—three other apprentices finally split, but I stayed. I don't want him ever to feel that what he did for me was wasted. Bill never knocked me—even when I'd go back to my old friends and was staying high all the time; he made me feel like a young Diego Rivera.

The studio was small; we all slept on mattresses on the floor.

"I had never read a book—all the way through—till I was eighteen. Bill would read stuff to me—Teilhard, Freud, all kinds of things I couldn't understand, beautiful stuff. I feel bad now thinking how many times I fell asleep while he was reading out loud. He told me about Michelangelo, Greek art, Chinese art, and about Rivera, Siqueiros, and Orozco—they interested me the most, which is what he'd hoped. Since then, I've really begun to study them.

"That Mexican mural art, that really hit me as what I always wanted to do. It was real art and it stirred the people to action. Meanwhile, to help out, I started working in a parking lot at nights, but I was messing up again—getting high, scoring, stealing cards, it was like a sickness.

"I remember the first time I met Corky—we were just a couple of kids off the street, and came right into his house, and he talked to us, really listened. He asked me to do the masthead for a paper he had then, *Viva*, but I never did it. Soon after, I got involved with the Young Democrats—I was window dressing for them, but I didn't know any better.

"I'd walk around as if I was another Siqueiros, and then Cesar Chavez invited me to come to California to work on his farmworker paper, *El Malcriado*—I had given him my biggest painting. I worked out there for four months; I put out a newsletter on what the strike was all about. When the trucks went by, we'd throw a roll of them up to the workers—we had them all ready, twenty to a roll. I also worked with Tijerina in New Mexico for eight months. I did posters in an isolated mountain cabin. At night we'd go out—it was pretty dangerous at that time—and put them up on posts, trees, and buildings.

"Then Carmelo Martinez, a Puerto Rican artist, and I hitchhiked to Mexico City—it took us two months; we'd stop in different towns and stay for a few days. We even met Siqueiros, and stayed in Mexico six months—it changed me as a person. It gave my art more direction—everything must be pointed toward liberation. The artist's relationship with his people is like that of a fish with water. In order really to survive, you have to be with the people, not alienated or individualistic; mural painting is public property and belongs to everybody. The artist who doesn't plunge into the water commits a kind of suicide; he will end up simply turning out a vehicle through which to sell products."

The Crusade also boasts of the first Chicano art gallery in the United States, manned by Carlos Santistevan, whose specialty is metallurgic art and sculpture. "An artist needs to be exhibited," Carlos said, guiding me through a striking range of new work. "It's usually very difficult, and some galleries even make a charge. I want to help Chicano artists, but I tell them, 'Do the things you have a feeling for.' "

He guided me to a large canvas alive with green and red and black. "Look at this," he exclaimed. "This woman couldn't get a job; she was painting her anger. She's not involved politically, but she has the best sense of what's happening in the community. See? The green snake is the symbol of greed. The Aztec bat—over there—is a devil. You see the dead people? I call them Span-Anglos. Success in this country involves a mental-spiritual prostitution."

Santistevan teaches art classes in the gallery several days a week, and seeks out artists whose work ought to be exhibited. Once it took him three weeks to locate one man's paintings, another two weeks to find the artist. Those represented are unknown in the fashionable galleries: one man whose sculpture is in the gallery works during the day in a foundry and does his sculptures at night. Another local artist, with several paintings on exhibition, is F. S. Crespin, a man in his eighties. "He's an authentic primitive," Santistevan explained delightedly. "He makes his own paints, then paints on cardboard, and makes his own frames. He has soul; looking at his pictures gives you a feeling of warmth."

I stopped in front of one of Santistevan's sculptures, a metal figure of a faceless man carrying a sign that says "Huelga."

" 'Huelga' simply means we're striking for our just due,"

Santistevan said. "Like a young friend of mine, who had won medals fighting in Korea. When he got back, he couldn't get a job, pay his rent, or his gas bill, or put clothes on his children. 'Overseas I was an American,' he told me; 'here I'm a dirty Mexican again. Over there I was fighting for freedom; here I don't have it.' So this metal figure wears a purple heart that has been broken. He's faceless, he can be anyone; 'he' is our people. We are all beautiful; so why should I give the figure a particular face?"

I asked Santistevan about his education, and how he had become involved in sculpture.

"I went to parochial school," he answered; "they told me I wasn't college material—so I learned how to weld in a trade school. See? The back of the man carrying the 'Huelga' sign is a large sheet of metal. I used an acetylene torch to shape it.

"You know," he confessed, "before I listened to Corky, I didn't realize how proud I was to be a Chicano. I was afraid that if I spoke Spanish, I'd be inferior; I didn't want to be a Mexican—they were lazy, dirty, illiterate, all that garbage. And now," he concluded proudly, "I'm helping people say what's in them, helping them find their own roots."

Gonzalez had already told me how important the change in the role of woman was in the Chicano movement. Martinez's wife, Sally, explained what this meant in terms of her own experience.

"I went into my marriage with blind faith," she said. "Then I went through a phase—many of the younger women had the same thing happen—when there seems to be a conflict. You see an opportunity for women to fill positions of leadership, but there's also the need to support your husband.

"I still feel that if a woman is going to be effective, it has to be through the man. Too many women in this society are competing with men—you can see this in their homes, in offices, even in sex. I'm not saying all the old ways were right, but I want to be doing what a real woman is supposed to do.

"It's hard for our young guys today—they're going to need strong women who realize it is their men and families that must come first. But having a family is no stopping point—you can watch your family grow, and see the way other children develop. They talk about 'liberation' but 'liberation' from what? The women in Cuba are pretty much equal to their men and have many of the same responsibilities, but they do run their homes. If her man is a revolutionist, the woman has to be, too. Even more may be demanded of her—understanding and courage."

As militant Chicanos entered into increased contact with black and white radicals, however, the question of "women's liberation" would become increasingly alive. Even now, the subject came up frequently at The Crusade.

"*Machismo* is what separates the man from the woman," Emilio Dominguez told me. "The man is the breadwinner, rulemaker, and controller of his family; that is as it should be. But without giving up our dignity, we want to show our wives how important they are—we have to help in raising the kids, we don't mind helping out, even changing a diaper once in a while. And we want woman to be involved; they have the right to play an important part in our work. Last year I asked women in The Crusade to come into our social service operation—what we call Band-aid."

What was Dominguez's opinion of birth control?

"I came from a family of eighteen—I never thought it was too many. My wife was raised in a family of fifteen—no one ever went hungry. How many make a family?

"I don't know, but it seems to me that what the Anglo is about with sex, there is no love involved, just pleasure. That book *Mandingo* tells me a lot here: the white man would get his white wife and black slave woman both pregnant. The black woman was supposed to supply food for the white baby, and the white woman had black male slaves for her pleasures—if a baby was born, nobody knew about it.

"My father depended on what he could make in the fields;

the more children, the more income. The real problem today is that a lot of babies aren't really accepted—twenty-four percent of the babies are born to unwed mothers. Birth control should be optional, to be used at the discretion of the parents. What does the priest know about my problems?"

Gonzalez, too, had thought a good deal about *machismo*, and explained his position one night at The Crusade in talking to a group of associates. "The women will fight and work with the men," he said. "They are developing into top leadership. For some men, this has been hard, as if attacking his *machismo*. But when a credit agent comes to the door of a Chicano house, who goes to the door to handle him? The old lady!—what does that say about *machismo*?"

A visiting priest at the center insisted that the Spanish had always been a father-dominated culture, whereas in America, among both whites and blacks, there were matriarchal tendencies. "Neither position is balanced. The Chicano tries to compensate for an inbalance he doesn't understand; since in fact the mother does exert considerable influence, all he thinks of is to appeal to his *machismo*. But like the Italians, the Chicano has always had a strong family unit, even though the man is often unfaithful."

Whatever remained unresolved on a theoretical level, the fact that a number of women were taking on leadership functions at The Crusade was surely significant. Theresa Romero, for example, wife of Ricardo Romero, was in charge of the 1969 summer school at The Center.

"Corky mentioned to the board members that school would be out soon," she recalled. "He told Virginia Salazar, 'Maybe this would be a good time for you to start your sewing class.' Then he said to Aeelia Espinoza, 'Maybe this would be a good time to start your Spanish classes.' That was all we needed to get started.

"We got ten sewing machines from the Opportunity School. They thought they could bring in one of their *gringo* teachers; they didn't expect us to have a qualified Chicano.

"There are also about fifty girls taking the class in Ballet Español—after all, Spanish dancing is an important part of our culture. The girls also run the nursery; they divide up the work so that they can also attend classes. And Tuesday night is *tortilla* night—girls come in to learn how to cook them; you'd be surprised how many come."

The success of the summer school, and the fact that two Chicano women had written its curriculum, would undoubtedly have continuing impact on the role of women in the emerging Chicano community.

After a week at The Center, I was puzzled by the fact that despite the anger and desperation of many of the key associates of The Crusade, the overall atmosphere was reassuring and friendly. Everyone was ready to drop what he was doing to help someone else; people indulged in heady rhetoric without becoming prisoners of ideology; there was evidence of genuine affection for Corky from young children and aged grandmothers, but no one seemed reluctant to interrupt him or disagree with him. I decided that the reason things worked out was that ultimately The Crusade operated as an extended family, just as chaotically, with just as much fierce pride, and perhaps somewhat more love than most other families.

Gonzalez, for example, despite all the tensions in the community and police surveillance, ran a completely "open" office, and people in The Crusade were taught to make use of his things as if they were their own. Personal copies of books he had brought to the office library did not remain stationary on the shelves, but were freely borrowed by those who needed them. Much of what went on would look terribly unstructured to the outsider, but the casual delight in improvisation was one of the very reasons for the success of the summer school, where a teenager would take over as teacher if a class got so large that it had to be divided, and one would not be surprised to see a boy of ten teaching the guitar to four younger children.

When Emilio Dominguez spoke about Chicano self-determination, he was also talking about family. "We're proud that our grandfathers and grandmothers are part of our families till they die. We don't send them off to rest homes and try to get rid of them; we're glad to take care of them. Anglos could learn from us. Here at the center, we opened up a room for the aged: about two dozen people came, all Anglos and blacks. No Chicanos came, because they weren't lonely."

Dominguez also insisted that the Chicanos had not yet experienced a severe generation gap, like the rest of the American culture. "You see fathers and sons together here at The Center. The father may have to give his son a haircut, but it is still father and son. Lots of Anglo kids come in—I don't mind, I listen. One of them, all dirty, with long hair, came all the way from New Jersey. He had asked his father to take him some place, but his father was too busy—said he'd give the kid the money. So the kid split.

"Here at The Center we try to get away from as many 'don'ts' as possible. People can feel free to walk into this office and use the desk—anyone can come and go as they wish. If they break down the door, it can be fixed."

Within the family, too, criticism of Gonzalez was perfectly acceptable, although an underlying loyalty became evident. Jack Lang, a Roman Catholic priest who helped out occasionally at The Center, thought Gonzalez was too outspoken. "He's not willing to give ground when he's made up his mind; he's stubborn. Sometimes he forgets that the majority of Chicano people prefer to live a quiet life; they've learned to put up with prejudice, maybe because of the fatalism in their background."

We were talking after a Sunday afternoon Mass that had been celebrated outside in the parking lot by another priest, Craig Hart, garbed in a *mestizo* counterpart of a chasuble, and with communicants receiving *tortillas* as well as wine. I asked Father Lang if Gonzalez was accepted as the leader by the Denver Chicano community.

"No," he answered thoughtfully, "there's no charismatic

leader who inspires our people. And besides, Gonzalez is no
Martin Luther King; he doesn't even try to be. Of course, I
don't know Corky very well as a person—probably not many
people do. But I've seen him operate in various crises. The
most important thing about him is that he is a compassionate
man, and his compassion is directed toward his own people.
When he was young he learned that you have to fight for
what you get, but he's more mature now. He knows there's
no point in confronting armed police with bare fists and pop
bottles.

"I am almost all Chicano, except for my name," Father
Lang explained. "The United States took our land in a
pseudolegal way; they posted tax notices in English with a
cutoff date. The people weren't told about it, and the land
was taken away from them. One time a Chicano made a tax
payment four hours late, and he lost several hundred thousand
acres. 'The Chicano Nation' really means the struggle for
identity of a nation within a nation. It doesn't mean that the
people don't want to be a part of the United States; it's a
desire for self-identity."

Father Lang shifted in his chair before going on, speaking
softly yet earnestly. His eyes were large and open, in search
of warmth for the soul that lay behind them. "I'm more of
an integrationist than a segregationist," he said. "But if I said
I have friends and roots in the Anglo community, they might
say I'm an Uncle Tom—a *tio taco*." He gestured almost im-
perceptibly with his hands. "I don't want to be integrated
into American technology, but into humanity. But I know that
Anglos are as much a part of humanity as browns or blacks
or anyone else. *La Raza* means a spirit that unites a people. It's
more than a political movement; it is the whole history and
culture. To give people pride is the important thing. They
do not need to feel like animals or be treated like animals;
they have a dignity."

Probably the pageant that The Crusade had created for
Christmas, 1968 would bridge many of the differences between

Father Lang and Gonzalez. As the latter described it, it was an updating of the story of Mary and Joseph journeying to Bethlehem for the first Christmas; in this version, they come to Denver. "First," Gonzalez explained, "they go to ask for lodging at the home of a well-known bigot, whom we mention by name. They are driven away and end up at the Hilton, where the manager chases them. A commercial Santa Claus says he's working *his* corner and for them to get off his block. Then they are arrested by a policeman for vagrancy. The judge turns them over to volunteer probation officers. They tell them what to do with their lives, and to come back the next Wednesday. But the probation officers become embroiled in a furious discussion among themselves because they're caught up in their personal problems. Next, Joseph and Mary go to the country club, where they're kicked out. Finally, they bed down in a Chicano home, where the people take care of them. And we had a banner over an arch that read, 'Chicano Power.' "

I understood that Gonzalez was not yet nationally known as a minority-group spokesman, but some of my informants suggested that he had special importance as a figure pointing to a new stage of the Movement, dependent less on names—often created overnight by the mass media—than on communities that had come together in dignity and self-help. In his office one afternoon, I asked Gonzalez about the other Chicano spokesmen.

"If you look at the Movement across the Southwest," he said, "you'll see that most of the leaders are depression babies. Chavez is forty-two. Tijerina is forty-three. I'm forty-one. As yet, there has been no real student movement; the students will take the ideas that have already been developed, and maybe they'll move them further than we can.

"Chavez is one of the most symbolic figures in the history of the Southwest. He's been able to survive, partly because he has one of the finest organizational minds in the country. Dealing with the economic level, and just with farm workers, he has become the embodiment of *la causa,* meaning the cause at all levels. What he's done has nationalized people, even though Chavez doesn't claim to be nationalistic.

"Reies Tijerina is a different sort of man. He's not pragmatic at all; he's willing to take action at any cost. His most important contribution is as a symbol of total resistance, preparing a revolutionary approach. He's chasing governors and scientists and forest rangers to make citizen arrests; and this becomes very positive. It may get more publicity than results, but it teaches the Mexican-American that leaders can be treated as equals; that they must be our servants, not our masters.

"For myself, I'm dealing in revolutionary thought. The white radical thinks he's heard it all before, but for him it's all guilt or just book knowledge. Pragmatically, we have to have the patience to relate to people on the basis they can understand. But I'm encouraged—why two years ago, I couldn't speak to my own people—or even my own family—the way you've heard me talking at some of our meetings."

Tentatively, I raised the issue of violence.

"I'm against the war in Vietnam," he said forcefully. "I'm against the hypocrisy of our intervention, the indiscriminate killing of civilians, the intervention of big brother who lays waste the countryside and rapes the women. Chicanos in particular have no business in Vietnam, fighting another minority group, a people who are poor and colored.

"The Establishment doesn't want to recognize that violence comes in many forms—poverty, oppression, racism. Cultural genocide against a people is also violence. The real violence in this country is police state violence against demonstrators.

"When I see the hunger of a child, I see violence. Violence is the destruction of human beings—mentally, physically, or spiritually."

It was only on one of our last drives through Denver, however, that I was able to place Gonzalez's words in the context of a young man growing up.

"I lived right there, in that house, thirty-six years ago,"

he said, pointing through the open car window. "The place burned twenty-nine years ago, and they're *still* renting it.

Gonzalez had been born on June 18, 1929. His mother, who was from Trinidad, in the southern part of Colorado, died when he was two. He lived with his father and three brothers in Denver, working during the summer in the fields as soon as he was able.

"My father made a pledge he would bring no woman into our house; he wanted to make us men. He was a miner; then he worked on the railroads. We learned to take care of ourselves, no baby-sitters; it was good training for a revolutionary. He was very strict. When I was little I didn't know who came first, my father or God. When we were in the fields, the rule was plain: if you didn't work that day, you didn't eat that night.

"My father taught us that we were Mexican. 'You have reason to be proud of your history; you have your heroes—we are a whole people. But living under the *gringo*, we've been taught we're failures. The Anglo expresses his racism even in the tone of voice.'"

Corky stopped the car again in what he identified as "skid row," pointing out the pawn shops and the bars where "you can get a double shot of wine for fifteen cents."

"We used to live in a condemned house halfway down the next block. We didn't know it was condemned until the guy downstairs left and the water was cut off—we'd been paying him all that time. Over there—that's the oldest Catholic church in Denver—is where I was confirmed. That other building—I used to sweep the gym there; it was on the second floor. Of course, I'd started fighting in the streets. Then I entered community center tournaments; I'd make five to fifteen dollars in an amateur fight and give my dad most of it."

We had crossed over to Denver's west side.

"I went to junior high school here," he said. "I was very quiet at school and loud at home. Even in high school, I acted very much Indian—I did my work and withdrew to my other world, the *barrio*. My brothers went into the service early, so I was very much on my own. My father worked nights, until two A.M.; most of my friends ended up being busted."

He pointed to a stone building on our right.

"That was the Methodist Community Center," he explained. "You know, I used to be the smallest guy in our group. I took it for granted I had to take beatings. But I developed my boxing at The Center—and they fired the guy who was taking care of us there, said he was contributing to delinquency. I realize now he was trying to be my friend; he used to box with me. He was looking around, picking out leadership to develop."

Gonzalez was still bitter about the racism of most of his teachers but remembered one woman teacher who had encouraged him in junior high because of his ability to get good grades. "She gave me my first tickets to go to a school play. I wasn't sure I could go because my clothes were so bad—I had to turn up the sleeves of my old suit coat. My pants were all worn, but an overcoat covered them. Another time, I was given a ticket to a Hi-Y dinner; I didn't know what fork to use. I was wearing girl's gumsole shoes—my brother found them junking, which is how I got most of my clothes."

We came to another corner, and he slowed the car again.

"Those are the cheapest projects in town—cement floors. Youth gangs used to fight each other here—the Wolf Group and the Dukes—now they're learning to fight the system instead. Revolutionary action has begun to take place—all these businesses are owned by absentee landlords, many of them Jewish. There was real confrontation not long back; the people had posters: 'Drive the Exploiters Out—Chicano Power.' They liberated that building—and that other one; I used to live there, on the second floor, with my sister and her husband, when I was ten years old." It was a simple brick building with a grocery store downstairs, an apartment above it, overlooking the street.

"We used to get arrested for walking down Cherry

Creek," Corky continued. "Some of the trees had wild plums then, and we'd catch minnows in the creek. And we'd liberate a lot of apples."

We circled back past the high school from which Gonzalez had graduated in 1945. "I was the only one in the family who graduated from high school," he said. "I worked and started college on my own money. I had top scholastic honors, but since I was a Chicano no one told me about scholarships; college wasn't considered for us. In high school I enjoyed reading poetry and philosophy, but my teachers didn't encourage me. Then, since I had taken classes in machine shop and mechanical engineering, I enrolled for a quarter in mechanical engineering at the University of Denver."

Gonzalez next tried to join the navy, but since his three brothers were all in the service, his father refused to sign the papers. Then, at nineteen, he turned to professional boxing—as he himself admits, "to make a fast success and get all the things society had deprived me of, and that I hadn't gotten out of school."

"I won sixteen or seventeen fights in a row and was rated in the top ten of the world. I managed myself, since I didn't trust anyone—the fighters put their heads on the line, and the managers put their hands out. In 1948 I fought fifteen main-event fights and lost only one; I was making fair money. Actually, even though I thought I wanted success, I had a kind of fear about money, probably from my father and what I thought of as the law of compensation. I didn't feel I deserved the money I was making—I'd give it away or lend it.

"The strange thing was that because I was always in training, I lived almost like a monk and had time for self-analysis. I was always dissatisfied: when I beat a guy, I felt sorry; if I lost, I felt dejected. The whole fight business—there was no consideration for the human being; I was just a machine. But when I quit, it was hard for awhile. I wasn't in the top ten any more. I still have scrap books, but, as I tell my kids, you can't eat press clippings, and the trophies don't chew too well, either."

In 1949 Gonzalez married Geraldine Romero; their eldest child is nineteen, their youngest is a four-year-old girl.

"When I was twenty-two, I bought a restaurant and bar business; a brother managed it. I opened a gym to teach kids to box, but it lost money. All kids were welcome but hardly any Anglo boys would come down to Larimer Street—I just had a few black kids, mostly Chicanos. Of course, when you become a restaurant owner in the *barrio*, you become an ombudsman in the community. I had run-ins with the police, put up bond for people, talked with the kids, even advised on marriages."

How had Gonzalez gotten into active politics?

"In 1955 I ran for councilman—forced a guy who was in his third term in the legislature into a runoff. Then I realized I had no chance because Chicanos weren't registered. I started a big voter registration drive and learned I could be an effective debater. The highest percentage of our people in Denver history turned out to vote; I lost, but I learned a lot.

"After that, I organized for John Carroll who was running for U.S. Senate. He was what they then called 'liberal Democrat'; he was supported by labor. I helped get out the vote in thirty-six precincts and was appointed a district captain—the first Mexican-American; my district included the areas I showed you, skid row, the projects.

"The whole deal was no good because we were in someone else's pocket. They would take care of you individually but did nothing for your people. But I worked at it till 1964; there had been only thirteen Chicano committeemen; when I left, we had close to ninety. I went to court, tried to help, get jobs for people, but I felt I wasn't accomplishing much—just an Anglo success symbol. I learned to work with the black community; I believed in that, even though some of our own people gave me a hard time for it because we weren't making much progress ourselves.

"About 1960 I started as a bonding agent. Within six months, I had taken the equity on my house and started my own bonding business; pretty soon it was the biggest in

Colorado. We broke down a lot of barriers, and five young Chicanos got established in the business. But human beings came first. No one else would take a drunk bond. I'd go out at three or four in the morning to get them out of jail; then I'd have to wake them up at seven, or eight to get them to court. Or take a guy to the hospital and wait for hours to get him committed."

I asked Gonzalez what had moved him from reform politics to nationalism.

"I finally admitted that our politics were strictly racist; blacks and Chicanos ran only in their own districts. At a Democratic meeting, I'd feel isolated and would sit with a black. And there were a couple of police brutality cases; we finally got a Chicano deputy sheriff, but the party hacks weren't interested in it. In 1963 we started Los Voluntarios as a Chicano organization; there were probably about a hundred hard-core members and many of them were still not nationalized. Hell, in the early years I was boxing, I was still reading Steinbeck, Whitman, Hemingway, Mailer, but didn't know my own writers—Lorca, Neruda, Jimenez. Anyway, I stopped dealing with prestige types and started with grassroots people. My friends were worried about threats against me, but I told them that this happens to anyone who stands up against the system.

"We had to teach the people not to fear anyone. One day a policeman who was six feet two inches tall, weighed two hundred thirty-five pounds, and had been drinking tried to beat a Chicano man with a club. I ran to help the Chicano, was able to hold off the blows, and got in a left to the policeman's face. When he fell, he broke his leg, and I was charged with assault and battery, even though the policeman had a long history of brutality. Fortunately, there were over thirty witnesses and I won a 'not guilty' verdict in court. One of my witnesses was an Anglo; the policeman had beaten him up because he hung around with Mexicans. Another witness was a black kid who called the police after this cop had beaten him; the police then let this cop work the kid over again. After that trial, the police would try every kind of harassment on me, but that cop hasn't dared get out of line. And even the harassment stopped after we got the community organized. The police don't want any martyrs, any Chicano Huey Newton. Because the movement could spread across the Southwest like fire. But our Selma will be in Texas—with those Texas Rangers and the landowners, it's not going to be nonviolent there."

Gonzalez served as chairman of the Denver War on Poverty, and when he began the Neighborhood Youth Corps many Chicanos were employed as counselors. It was after leaving government-sponsored poverty work—amid vague allegations, denied by the O. E. O. in Washington—that he followed up a decision to incorporate the first Chicano civil-rights organization by naming it The Crusade for Justice. "It was a cold night," he remembered, "April 29, 1966; about two thousand of our people came out. We had three main incentives: first, civil rights; second, social services to provide the glue to bring people together and meet their needs; and third, an emphasis on culture to help the people understand themselves."

A little more than two years later The Crusade was able to acquire Calvary Baptist Church for its headquarters. "Our people know it belongs to them. They painted and scrubbed it; step by step, we're getting it paid off. We put on my play, *The Revolutionist*, thirty-nine times in colleges, churches, and conferences, to raise money. Now The Center is a stop-off point for Chicanos crossing the country."

There was a smile of accomplishment. "I can hang around more, and not go to so many conferences. I'm needed here, for leadership training. And with less traveling around, maybe I can find time for more writing—poetry, plays, maybe a novel. With The Center here, I can involve my whole family; they're all a part of it. Too many people in social action keep their families at home—the wife gossiping on the phone, the children watching John Wayne movies on TV; they're taking one step forward and two backward. I don't want any generation gap. My wife's mother, Mrs. Romero, is eighty-four—she's the one who sings all the *cantos* for us; she'd march if we'd let her."

My last night at The Center, Gonzalez's oldest daughter, who had married earlier in the year at the Chicano youth conference, telephoned from Michigan, where she was living with her husband. She didn't have a copy of one of her father's poems and wanted him to read it to her. Gonzalez had written the poem, *Adios, Miguel*, about a ten-year-old Chicano boy who had died. Gonzalez's daughter had come to know a family in Michigan whose son was seriously ill and wanted to share her father's poem with them. Corky read it slowly, line by line, and hung up. The experience behind the poem still moved him. "Miguel died here soon after his tenth birthday; he had had many operations for his head. The boys always helped him up and down the stairs at The Center; they made him part of everything—he even came to the boxing classes. I read this poem at his graveside. He was buried in a *chaleco*, his choir robe. When they lowered the casket into the grave, the kids gave ten mighty shouts of 'Chicano power.' "

I asked Corky about his other writing.

"Like many other young Chicanos, I couldn't speak good Spanish," he recalled. "I thought that after a while it wouldn't bother me, but it does—Spanish is as much a part of us as our name or our religion. When I read the best Anglo writers, I knew I wasn't yet prepared to write art. But I worked hard— I sold a piece to a Catholic magazine, and another editor liked a story I did and sent it to the *Saturday Evening Post*. They rejected it; they said the writing was good, and the story, but there were no Anglo characters. A month later, they ran a story with no Anglo characters, written by an Anglo!"

I already knew about his long poem, *I am Joaquim*, which was being used in Chicano Studies Programs throughout the Southwest. Another poem, *America! America!*, grew out of his experience with the March on Poverty in Washington in 1968. A year earlier, he had written the play, *The Revolutionist*, set in a large Southwestern city, in the early 1950's. The setting is the living room of a slum home, and the dedication is: "To my father, whom I now understand."

"The play is human, sometimes entertaining, and very fast," Gonzalez told me. "Italians and Japanese came to see the play and cried. A man is destroyed, almost, by the society. Chicanos cheer, because they know what he was fighting. Anglos enjoy it at first, then they don't understand, and suddenly they see the man destroyed. Different schools want copies for social studies. When you read it, pay attention to the epilogue."

He showed me a clipping from *The Denver Post:*

> *Gonzalez is concerned that while "literature can be a potent social weapon," the Spanish-surnamed minority has not yet had a James Baldwin or an Oliver Lafarge to speak of. Meanwhile,* The Revolutionist *has had to turn away customers, there have been requests to bring the play to other parts of the state, and the cast has received standing ovations. But what impresses Gonzalez is that children and teenagers in the audience are attentive. "That's the greatest tribute," he said. "If we reach the kids, we've accomplished something."*

In 1968 Gonzalez wrote another play, *A Cross for Maclovio.*

"It's about a middle-aged civil-rights leader who is going through the conflict of turning over his work to someone else," he explained. "The play has many elements: the feelings of his wife, religious overtones, the meaning of life in the face of death, the messianic complex of some men.

"Why does Malcolm X keep on when he knows he's going to die? Or Christ? Or Gandhi? Or Martin Luther King, going to the top of the mountain? Maclovio is still trying to rouse his people, even though he knows what's in store for him, and that his wife will be left with nothing but memories, no security.

"I wrote it in two days, then I went back and restructured it. But I haven't had time to go back to do any more work on it. The wife's closing statement is a castigation of society; there can be no way out. There's a white liberal in the play, always talking about structure and political realism. We see all the phonies in the movement—last year's militants.

"At the end of the play, as car lights go by, they cast the shadow of a cross. But there'll be no crosses for Maclovio, because he's just a man."

I sensed the personal anguish contained in the play's conclusion, and was reminded of the evening in The Crusade's meeting room when I had been disturbed to see Gonzalez address the audience while standing with his back to an open window, which faced an alley. I asked him if this had been prudent, in the light of what he knew about the violence in American society; he said he was usually more careful.

"But the man who comes to kill me takes a fifty-percent chance of getting killed himself," Gonzalez said evenly. "Being a martyr seems less productive to me than living. Besides, you can kill a man, but not a philosophy he has set in motion in people's minds. When two cops take a Chicano or a black man out of a bar, and a hundred people walk out to demand a reason, that means Malcolm X is *alive*—that's Malcolm X *speaking*."

He handed me a copy of *The Revolutionist* to read that evening, and we said good-night. Back in my room, I turned directly to the epilogue, in which Joaquim must make a painful reaffirmation of spiritual integrity:

> *Here I stand before the court of justice, guilty for all the glory of my Raza, to be sentenced to despair. . . . Mejicano, Español, Latino, Hispano, Chicano, or whatever I call myself, I look the same, I feel the same, I cry*

and sing the same. . . .
My blood is pure.
I am Aztec prince and Christian Christ.
I shall endure!
I shall endure.

3

The Commune
and Women's Liberation

We all live temporary lives, he said. We think that just for now
things are going badly, that we have to adapt just for now, and
even humiliate ourselves, but that all this is temporary. Real life
will start someday. We prepare to die with the complaint that
we've never really lived. Sometimes I'm obsessed with this idea. You
live only once, and for this one time you live a temporary life,
in the vain hope that one day real life will begin. That's how we
exist. Of those I know, I assure you, no one lives in the present.
No one thinks that what he does every day is anything but temporary. No one is in a position to say, "From now on, from whatever
day this is, my life has really started." Even the ones who have
power and take advantage of it, believe me, live on intrigues and
fear. And they're full of disgust with the prevailing stupidity. They
live temporary lives too. They're waiting just like everyone else.

Ignazio Silone, *Bread and Wine* (New York, Atheneum House, Inc.,
1962).

The neat, white two-story house stood behind pine trees in the middle of the block in a town housing one of the state universities of California. The street on which the house faced was racially integrated and rather quiet, although not far from one of the busiest arteries in town.

It was a late summer afternoon, and three men—two in work clothes, the other stripped to the waist and wearing short trunks—were playing ball on a large stretch of lawn adjoining the driveway. When they saw me arriving, the men stopped their game and walked over to greet me. We shook hands and climbed the steps of the porch; the mailbox listed seven names.

Just beyond a battered screen door lay the main room of the house. When the four of us walked in to join four young women, a baby boy, three dogs, and at least two cats, the garbled assortment of furniture seemed to close in on us, and the room was suddenly quite small.

Seated in a straight chair close to my right side, someone was smiling encouragingly, it turned out to be Amanda. Halfway across the room, looking very much like Sandy Dennis in films, stood Laura, leaning against a table filled with books, hi-fi equipment, and enough paraphernalia for a mod-antique shop. To my left, seated on the floor, Peter distractedly shook his unruly head of hair and scowled. On an overstuffed old couch, Jen turned unblinking eyes at this stranger in their midst, and held her month-old son. On the far side of the room, leaning back precariously in a squeaking chair, Willie stared imperturbably at me.

"You seem nervous," Amanda said, still smiling warmly. "Is something the matter?"

"Yes," I replied. "My back hurts badly, I feel very tired, I'm alone with this tight group of people who belong together and suddenly all of you are somehow threatening to me. It's not your fault, but it's how I feel."

Each in his or her own way quickly reassured me that I was indeed welcome. Soon we were laughing and talking, and

Hibbie got up to prepare hot tea for those of us who wanted it. By then it had been explained that six of these men and women comprised couples who were married to each other: Hibbie and Peter, Jen and Chuck, and Amanda and Willie. Laura was single. John, whom everybody insisted was a commune baby and not to be identified narrowly with his biological parents, was the child of Jen and Chuck.

The house managed to hold everybody comfortably. On the first floor, in addition to the main room, was a small dining room, a crowded kitchen, a study (with categories), a bathroom, and the single rooms occupied by two of the couples, Hibbie and Peter, and Amanda and Willie. On the second floor, Jen and Chuck occupied the front bedroom, Laura's room looked over the large backyard, and there was a second bathroom and a closet. In the basement, was a recreation room (the TV set was here), an art room for Hibbie, a guest sleeping area screened off by hanging blankets, and much-needed storage space.

The commune was very new, scarcely four months old, but had slowly been coming together over a period of several years as relationships between the various people in it had formed. The opportunity to talk with socially involved, deeply caring people who were on the threshold of commune life—to find out why they desired it and what they anticipated in their mutual development—promised to be even more instructive than a study of an older, more settled group.

These pages are primarily a report on long, candid, and completely private talks I had with each of the seven members of the commune. What has been reproduced is what each of the seven people had to say, as our dialogue progressed.

Afterward, in a meeting between myself and the whole commune, pseudonyms were selected—finally by each person for himself, but only after considerable group discussion for all seven of the people. Some names seemed to fit certain individuals—that is, in terms of the peculiar imagery of names and the real personalities of people seated in that room—better than others. For myself, at least, Amanda conjures up a picture that curiously and nicely fits the young woman who bears that name in these pages; as for Jen, Laura, and Peter, they are somehow more successful pseudonyms for the people involved than are Hibbie, Willie, and Chuck. Chuck, in fact, said he didn't like his name, but none of us could seem to find a better one. As for Peter, I could not help but tell him jokingly, that his name might suggest to some people that he was the Rock, the primal figure, in the establishment of the commune.

The commune itself also has a name, a fitting and estimable one, but it wants no personal publicity at this time, nor did we feel any compunction to establish a pseudonym. In addition, in order to maintain the commune's anonymity, I have taken the liberty of altering certain other specific references, but none of these affect the basic details of the group's experience. The members of the commune were also concerned as to how the individual conversations I had conducted would be organized. They strongly resisted the ordinary usage of coupling married people—hence, to report successively my sessions with Hibbie and Peter, for example, would be in the tradition of referring simply to "Mr. and Mrs. Thomas Jones." In order, therefore, to comply with their wish to stand within these pages as individuals, I decided to alphabetize the pseudonymical names, which meant beginning with Amanda and ending with Willie.

Animated and full of energy, Amanda speaks very, very quickly but her thoughts are racing far ahead of her words. Exceptionally good-looking, she wears simple clothes that do not attract special notice to herself. She wears her black hair pulled back tightly over her head, has expressive liquid eyes, and gestures almost constantly with her hands as she speaks. A nervous laugh breaks into almost every other sentence, and she smiles more often than most other people. In our group session at the end, I told the commune that with her distinct Jewish cultural identity and the central role she played in the commune's formation, for me Amanda represents "Mother Earth."

"I never had to go through the trauma of realizing your

parents are maybe not really good people," she told me. She is twenty-three, the only child of an eastern advertising man and a social worker; having completed her M. A., she is now working on her Ph. D. in sociology. (It soon developed that an overall concern, both existential and professional, in the area of sociology ties nearly everybody in the commune together.)

"Yes, the whole thing formed around Willie and me more than anybody else," Amanda said, laughing. "We were the central focus because we knew everybody." After the commune formally came together the previous May, at the end of the school year, Amanda and Willie went to Africa for three months to engage in field work; they had just returned. "Our being away made us important—as if we could have solved all the problems they were dealing with. The whole thing needs time—what we're doing in the commune is clearly a political action. We have set up a unit that does the job of a family, or several families, and defies the social requirements set by society at large of what is called the nuclear family: the concept of competition, established roles for men, women, even for children, and economic rules. We're trying to seize control of our own lifestyles. For example, work in the world outside the commune should be to support someone in it to do what he wants.

"Frankly, I'm not interested in living in a nuclear family. It's the form dictated by capitalism, the most useless social unit, and also the least friendly. Your children are taught to group up in competition. All this is reflected in the usual brittleness of a family. That doesn't mean that communes are the answer for everybody and everything. A lot of people should consider them, though, because it's very liberating for middle-class kids to give up some property concepts."

Amanda paused to bring up a dilemma which she felt the commune had not sufficiently confronted. "Not that we've completely overcome our own formation. The things in our basement reflect an economic unit I'm opposed to."

In the basement of the house, I learned, were stored many former individual and couple possessions, along with many presents, especially recent ones for young John. I remembered being in the kitchen one morning when the mail came, bringing an expensive and lavishly wrapped gift for the baby, and triggering a baffled and serious discussion of group values.

"Damn it," Amanda continued, "you can't afford a cultural revolution unless you can afford to give away that stuff in the basement, those three electric mixers, four electric toasters, two dozen towels, and three stereo sets. How can you say 'Form a commune and give up your worldly goods' to a black woman in Harlem who supports six kids? She's going to have to solve other problems first before there's a cultural revolution in *her* view."

The question of these used, and presently stored, possessions posed a number of ironies. For example, one tough practical problem concerned who was to wash the dishes stacked in the kitchen sink, and on what kind of schedule they were done. A dishwasher would be an immediate solution, but the commune wishing to move toward greater simplicity in lifestyle, fiercely resisted the intrusion of yet another middle-class convenience that could ultimately be a trap. "Look at the status thing of having an air-conditioner," Amanda said.

I knew that Amanda and her friends possessed considerable social and political awareness. Would concentration on the development of the commune mean turning one's back on broader political issues?

"The outside world is a pretty big, bad place. I've been in and out of political movements—civil rights and Vietnam. It's no longer interesting to invest any time in liberal communities doing liberal reforms. Even in the past, I was never at ease in all that activity, even when politically convinced that it might be accomplishing something.

"My program for the Black Panthers wouldn't be a *commune*. They're in a different position and what they need to do is probably very different from what I need to do for myself.

"Actually, it's hard for me to talk about politics right now. I'm not very clear about it—this summer changed my head around. I'm going to have to find out to what extent I can work with any political group.

"But I think women's liberation groups are of primary importance to any female who wants to be conscious at all. I've been in three of them, all built around an analysis of the role of women in this society. I'm beginning to understand some ways in which I am personally oppressed. But, I'd like to get away from just talking with student women and find out how ordinary housewives and working girls look at some of these things. After all, my own home life isn't really chauvinist."

I told Amanda how I wished that she might be able to meet with two groups of women outside her immediate experience who were wrenching themselves free from restricted roles: Chicano, or Mexican-American women, representing the nation's second largest ethnic or racial minority, and Roman Catholic nuns. This reminded her how, as a child of six, she had wanted to be Roman Catholic. "This was because all Catholic girls were brides, getting married to God, and had white dresses. They were going to make their first communion. I was very conscious that I had to defend the fact that I was an atheist." She also told me about an incident in sixth grade, when a teacher, during a discussion on the subject of religion, asked Amanda to stand up and describe "what a Jew is." Eleven-year-old Amanda rose at her desk and replied: "I don't know; I'm an atheist," and was temporarily suspended from school for her seeming lack of propriety. "I was conditioned as a child that all religions were mythology," Amanda explained, "and I read a little bit about all of them. But when I was twelve, I went through an experience of trying to pray—because I was afraid. It lasted for three months.

"An evangelistic lady from a Protestant missionary Sunday-school sect called on my family. We were the only atheists in the block. My family let her take me off to what was called Board and Jelly school. They used the Bible and felt boards: it all seemed pretty and a bit interesting at the time."

Did Amanda want to be a mother?

"I really dig kids and want to have some of my own," she replied. But without having to be 'somebody' *or* 'somebody's mother.' In the commune, we should have enough mental and emotional strength not to give in to the meaning of American motherhood and being a housewife."

Amanda was aware of differences within the group, which needed to develop a language that would include them all. "Four of us," she continued, "are overly trained in sociology. I wish Jen didn't think we were condescending to her. We're not, but we do talk a different language. I tend to analyze the social-psychological relations constantly developing, shifting, breaking down. Of course some of the others don't feel the same need to constantly talk things over.

"I'm not going to give up me; so I'll keep on being myself. But that doesn't mean being oppressive, and saying 'unless we talk things over, I can't live here.' I've still got to learn not to exude intensity. The fact is, I used to play mother too much. The trick is to be friends without doing people head liberating favors that make them children."

I led the conversation back to the beginnings of the commune.

"Last May, when school was over, we all sort of said, 'Jesus Christ, it's such a bloody shame to leave. Why don't we live together?' We decided not to let our friendships get generated out of existence by our jobs.

"A good measure of how it works is how comfortable Laura, as a single girl, is living here with the rest of us who are married. The question for the future is: how many others like Laura can join us?

"You know a lot of married people—especially wives—just relate as the other person in a couple. I know I'm an individual, and Willie rarely stifles me. It's probably the other way around, because I talk more. It's important for us to evolve a lifestyle that permits other people who are different to be comfortable with us. I don't want to get into being a bunch of married couples who share a house. I used to use the word community a lot. Now I don't care what 'it' is called, so long as it is home."

Two single men, Amanda told me, had considered joining the commune. One of them had decided that at least for now he could not correlate his sexual activity with living in the house with the three married couples and Laura. He would simply not yet feel free to express himself, with his drives and attitudes, in such a setting.

It was necessary to raise the obvious question: what about the possibility of sex with someone in the commune other than her husband?

"I would like to keep an open mind," Amanda answered evenly. "There are some things liberating for me as an individual. For example, if I'm tired and dirty, I can step into a shower with someone else, another man or woman living in the commune. That's not a boundary that stops me at this point. But I don't know what will happen to me or to other people I'm living with if others decide to cross a boundary before I do. It then becomes the matter of my reaction to other people's boundary systems.

"But males and females living together always relate in a sexual manner. A year and a half ago, I was terrified that Willie might leave me. Before we were married, I'd gone through a lousy romance that lasted too long, so I needed to be the one and only. Today it's different. Time seems more important to me—I might be more offended by someone taking up Willie's time, like I do now, rather than simply his body.

"The barriers ahead of us aren't so frightening. Growing constantly means permitting possibilities, so we can change. Willie and I have learned we can be alone a lot and dig together. Now we want to try another lifestyle, to put our human relations ahead of our economic possibilities, whether it's a question of jobs, or being parents, or buying things. I remember how my family always wanted to set up a retirement plan with their friends and live together. So this has roots, but it's something new."

Amanda was especially fearful of the growing polarization in American society.

"It's harder now to tow a middle line. You know, I used

to be considered a strange girl because I had straight hair and wore sandals. Now hippies feel I'm square. Drug-heads would have a different commune than ours; we're not hung up about the drug scene but whether the dishes will be done—we've got different concerns.

"Something has to be done to keep people sane. Sane and happy. The symbols of our alienation have already been coopted. You can go into almost any store and, for forty dollars, look like an East Village kid. Everybody writes about experimental lifestyles. Everything that was way out has been coopted and belongs to mass culture. But maybe, if all this gets through to people, it's a good thing."

She described a fraternity house party on the third floor; for her it was an example of the square, a situation in which pot was used in abundance.

"In a sense, there's no longer a possibility of being an individual, who can read and act different from the mass culture. As Marcuse says, when you can find Marx in your local drugstore on a paperback shelf, Marx has been neutralized. Ironically, we found Marcuse's own book, *One-Dimensional Man*, in the book rack on a boat.

"We can hope the revolution is coming, whatever it means. At least there's something happening now that is non-violent and nonpolitical, something social, concerned with lifestyles. This commune may bust up, and we'll have to form another one. A lot depends on how much people want to seize the power involved in running their own lives."

I continued to probe the problem of how building a commune was a political act.

"Well, the answer is going to have to be political because it has to do more than free me. I'm not going to be fully free until everybody in this country has some say in their own lifestyles. It's a question for everyone, not just for blacks in the ghettos, or Chicanos.

"There must be solidarity with those who are more oppressed than we are. But white people aren't going to be the main force in the coming political shakeup. We may participate when and if it happens. I'd want to. But I'm down on the idea of cadres—it's an Old Left scene, and I don't like it."

It wasn't long before Amanda came back to her favorite subject, women's liberation.

"Without talking jargon or politics, you've got to say that revolution is necessary for any woman who opens her eyes, and sees what her 'womanly role' really amounts to.

"But women's liberation is far from an antimale movement. Hopefully, we're redefining both sexual roles. We want to free the man who is losing his humanity too, slaving away for higher productivity, bringing his paycheck home to the little woman." Amanda smiled, recalling her childhood. "You know, I had a daddy who was a gentleman, and who opened doors for a woman. That whole chivalrous myth must go. It's been exploded, but ramifications of it are still around us. Even now, so much of what's written still reflects the idea of woman as a passive sexual object. What males can look forward to from women's liberation is humane and satisfying relations with persons of the opposite sex who will be *people*."

Chuck, the most outwardly friendly member of the commune, is also, at twenty-six, the oldest. He and his wife, Jen, are the parents of John, the commune's baby. Chuck's temporary sense of defeat, because of flunking oral examinations for his doctoral degree, shows in his eyes. He is caught up in a real struggle to find identity, not just for himself, but for his wife, his son, and everybody in the commune; his personal dilemma is now shared by the others. His desk inside the study is unused, and he wears working clothes as a constant reminder of his present—probably temporary—job as a mechanic. Chuck expresses himself with tremendous honesty, rare directness, and an intuitive feeling for words. Although his manner suggests restlessness and alienation, a personal warmth and easy sense of humor are never absent.

"We have consciously tried to put together an ideology,"

Chuck began. "Peter is especially concerned about this. You see, we all suffered from the nuclear family—all our families went through the depression, then came their obsession with possessions—a car, a house, and dominance.

"So, for us, the next question was how not to do *that*. The answer was the commune. Jen was already pregnant when we talked about these things. We didn't want John to live with just two people who would be authority figures. In the commune, everybody would be an authority figure, but not in the same way as in the nuclear family. I thought it was really cool; in fact, we all came up with it as the only thing to do."

What kind of family life had Chuck known growing up at home?

"I had a horrible experience of a very typical family. My father is a racist and extremely anti-intellectual. His family was once rich but, because of the depression, he was forced out of college when there was no money. My mother came from a very insular little town in the East. They got married, and he has worked himself up to one step below an executive level sort of thing.

"Now he's thinking about getting old. He says he's been fulfilled with what he did, but I look at how he worked his ass off in that shluck job, and it's completely unsettling, plus the fact that he supports the war in Vietnam and talks about sending the 'niggers' back to Africa.

"And he's supported by my mother. They're complex; very, very middle class. So I grew up with strange sexual understandings about what it was to be a male, a young boy. My mother said she didn't know what sex was until she got married when she was twenty-four. Living at home, I was part of the young-kid-in-the-high-school scene and attended a fancy white suburban school where ninety percent of the students went to college."

Religion was a primary aspect of his family's understanding of itself, Chuck explained, and had also played a curious role in his own life.

"My mother is Jewish and my father is a Methodist," he said. "I can't stand the Christian Playhouse thing—playing at going to church. My mother and father go all the time. But when she had a bad heart attack and the hospital where they sent her was located in the ghetto, all she could talk about was her paranoid fear that black people would come and burn it while she was there.

"My parents consider themselves seriously religious people with the right to make judgments about things being blasphemous. 'Blasphemous' is one of my father's favorite terms. Any attack on the concept or myth of God is 'blasphemous.'

"When I was a freshman in college, I had a sincere desire to believe in God, and got involved in religious-based civil-rights groups. You know, 'Racism is bad because it is wrong.' I spent part of a summer during college in a religiously sponsored program in a ghetto doing youth gang work. I was going to help those poor blacks because I was white and therefore had something to give. It was very Christian to be for black people then.

"Oh, I was even going to be a minister, but that didn't last more than a couple of years. My closest friend—who also became a sociologist—was seriously going to be a minister, too. Now, as then, he's hung up on ideological systems. I started reading Peter Berger, one of my cultural heroes. He knows enough about the religious systems of the Western world to do a good analysis."

I wanted Chuck to say more about the initial relationships that led him to the commune.

"Jen and I married when we both graduated from college," he explained. "At first, we lived as the typical white middle-class suburban couple on the way up. I remember when, in our second year of marriage, we were in an apartment complex chock-a-brim with the other young people on the make. We didn't like it. Then, as a normal academic, I went somewhere else for my Ph.D., and when we came here, by sheer luck, we got in a co-op through Jen's cousin. There were twenty-one guys and two married couples. Amanda and Willie were in one apartment, we in the other. Amanda and Willie had also lived singly in co-ops when they were undergraduates. As a point of information, our old co-op now has women as well as guys. Jen and I both found the co-op was a liberating experience. We weren't afraid of it because each of us had had some experience communally.

"All of us who are now in the commune have become alienated from the professional academic life that the university told us we were supposed to live. Previously, I would internalize my feelings—I was going to be a typical liberal humanitarian sociologist, writing for journals and living in suburbia. I wasn't going to be radical."

Chuck recalled how, over many a meal together during the co-op days, plans for the commune slowly took form. Then came a personal crisis when he failed to pass his preliminary examination for the Ph.D. "I wrote some glib answers," he said, "offended my superiors by telling them the truth—well, you know, the system has negative feedback. I was temporarily out of the program."

Presently, while deciding whether or not to return to the Ph.D. program at the university, Chuck is working as a car mechanic for about one hundred dollars a week. He was quite frank, however, in admitting that he missed teaching. "I enjoy interacting with a class. That's where my happiness is. The decision I must make isn't whether I want to become a teacher but whether or not to finish up the school thing. If I'm properly humble, it will be O.K. at the university. But I didn't expect to fail the prelims. It shook me badly. Those guys see the department as grinding out products they create and I didn't work out well for them."

We were in the study; it was evening and Chuck was relaxing after his day's work. In the dining room, Amanda was using a small sewing machine. Jen, Willie, and Hibbie were in the living room with John. Downstairs, Peter looked at television. Laura was out on a date.

"We're still interacting a lot with America," Chuck told

me. "We eat, look at the media, ride on the roads. But we're trying out alternative lifestyles. Talking has to end somewhere."

Chuck's attitudes toward women's liberation were extremely positive. "The women are essentially right," he declared. "You know, they've pointed out some incredible similarities between the relations of whites and blacks, on the one hand, and those of men and women, on the other. Men have been acting chauvinistic, dominating, possessive—including me. As the male, I was making decisions that exploited women, but it had to be pointed out to me, to take just one example, that women are really fucked academically. There—fucked—that's a chauvinistic term."

What about the likelihood of crossing sexual lines and couple units in the life of the commune?

"We all expected not, although we don't talk about it much. If we try to start out immediately on that level, it can only be disruptive, causing too many problems. I associate sex with intimacy—at this point I can handle it with only one person at a time. I'm a product of my background. I'd have to grow more. If we tried it now, it would be artificial. Many people automatically assumed that some of this was happening just because of living together, and this started us thinking and talking about it.

"For me, there's the guilt factor. I'd feel guilty about being unfaithful to Jen. That's part of my background coming out of the nuclear family structure. Here, we're trying to break down our identities as units, but we were preformed as units before we met. We were all married before the commune began, except Laura. The term 'withdrawal into coupling' is wrong. It's not that.

"We're getting over self-consciousness and beginning to feel like a family. Wearing underwear around the house is not an issue. A couple of times I've been lying on the bed without any clothes on when someone came in the room looking for something—it didn't bother either of us. But I don't like the idea of our trying to relate to each other artificially. I don't think it's possible for us to say 'Let's screw' or 'Let's all take our clothes off.' "

I remembered Amanda mentioning two young men who decided not to join the commune.

"They were going to come in," Chuck said, "and then they didn't, because of this sex thing. They're caught up in the young-single-man-scene. The whole dating syndrome is an extremely isolating thing for these guys. Again, it's chauvinistic. They didn't think they could make it in a community. These guys really feel they have to do it alone.

"A lot of this is the *Playboy* influence. Most of the women I respect and trust complain about it. It's a shame the way people are forced to play roles by the media."

I mentioned a student friend of mine in Connecticut who was living with nine other people (they were five men, all of whom had burned their draft cards, and four women); he had told me that he felt married to everybody—the eight other people—in the commune. Did Chuck understand such an attitude, and did he share it?

"No, I don't feel married to everybody. We're not yet, to be honest about it. It's something we're heading toward, in the sense of accepting responsibilities toward each other that are still beyond what we have here. But I can't put that into words. I don't really know what that means yet. Permanence is another factor. We talk about being together for a long time, maybe for the rest of our lives. But the only thing that's certain is that we're all here together to be together for a while."

Chuck gave voice to a familiar mixture of political concern and deep disillusionment.

"The old system of organizing ourselves is becoming disfunctional. I used to think it was enough to be against something: to protest, to try the legal way. Now we've found out that you don't change shit by laws. So we're into trying to find out how we can make a real change. Like racism in America, which is one of the key factors of capitalism and the consumer society. Look at what's happened to the white working class. Because of the incredible increase in production, they don't have it so badly, just because they aren't starving, and they don't seem to realize how many still *are*.

"One of the factors about my own liberation was the war in Vietnam. As one of the privileged middle-class white kids, I stayed out by staying in school. Some other kids had to go, and maybe get killed. I can't forget that."

Chuck got up, stretched, and went into the kitchen to get a jug of red wine. The sound of a TV comedy program, with its artificial canned applause, came up the basement stairs as he returned with two glasses. He meant the wine as a cheerful note but his mind was still on Vietnam. "I could go into a depressive thing for a while," he reflected, "and if I were alone, I probably would. People in the commune know this and are making an effort to help me."

I asked Chuck how he felt about his son being a commune baby.

He sat back in his chair and thought silently for a moment.

"Jen and I weren't sure about John. Since he's our child, we thought we should take the most responsibility for him during bad times. I felt bad about trying to sleep while she fed him, but otherwise I would have been dragging myself around at work.

"I remember the day Amanda and Willie came back; Hibbie had been feeding John. I felt she was doing a nice thing for us. I said, 'I'll take him off your hands.' About an hour later, Hibbie came up and was actually angry.

"Hibbie and Amanda felt I was setting myself up as if I was John's owner, by assuming that my responsibilities were primary. They felt he was as much their child as mine. You see, I was feeling 'thankful' to them, and that was wrong. They reminded me how John is a commune baby—and *that* was the issue."

Hibbie, who is twenty-three and married to Peter, seems the most intense member of the commune. Her views are clearly formed, hard and indestructible, and she communicates them with straight-to-the-point directness. She had long known various people who had lived in intentional communities, mostly Quaker ones, and the community idea (without religion) had always appealed to her. It is hard to account for, but after talking with her for a while, I suddenly realized there was no one at all like her in the commune. An artist, Hibbie also teaches in a day-care center.

"Yes, I've been interested in Quakers and pacifism for a long time," she told me. "It was a very romantic kind of thing. Nonviolence as a technique seemed very beautiful. But I've decided it isn't valid for this world, given the realities.

"Revolution is inevitable. It's not going to be a bunch of white radicals running around. On a world scope, oppressed peoples are going to change the whole design, instead of being run by a small group of white Europeans and Americans. Of course, the repression is going to get a lot worse before there is any change."

Hibbie is on good terms with her family. "My parents are both Stevenson liberals, liberal in a very good sense of the word. They taught me certain things and didn't back down when I took them at their word. But I didn't follow their advice to go to one of those classy eastern women's colleges— I wanted to get away from all that elitism and snobbism.

"My family has Jewish blood but they're all atheists. At first they sent me to Hebrew school, but when at the age of ten I told them 'It's all shit,' they said 'okay.' They're humanists, whatever that means."

Hibbie did not accept any writers or philosophers as idols, though she mentioned Kurt Vonnegut as someone whose humor she could "*relate* to." As for politics, despite her grim prediction that without basic reorientation of policy the U.S. would get into more Vietnams, women's liberation was of primary importance. "Of course, the black militants are completely right in what they're doing, but the woman thing more directly involves *me*. In one sense, the political action of the commune *is* women's liberation—you know, the lack of sexual differences. I believe there is no ultimate emotional difference between men and women. So for me the commune is living a political idea. There can be no radical change without sexual change, without men and women being equal. Right now women are socialized, even more than men are, to have certain things *represented* in them, in order to make them certain kinds of people."

What things, I asked Hibbie, and *what* kinds of people?

"Peter and I have been trying to figure out if there is a difference between men and women, apart from the obvious physical differences. 'If she's emotional,' she's a woman. *Or,* 'if he's such-and-such, he's a man.' But when we look at our relationship, and that of close friends, this sort of thing didn't make sense. In most good relationships I know, people relate as people, and aren't afraid to be masculine or feminine, if that's the way they feel. Masculine and feminine are only what society defines them to be.

"But all the pressure goes the other way: a woman is supposed to define herself in terms of her man. From the beginning, she's taught she will meet a man, who will be her husband, and give her children. And if two women are friends, there's always the understanding that if they are planning to do something, and one of their husbands calls, he automatically comes first. This contradicts a real human response."

Hibbie smiled a little at her own intensity, and I asked her what she foresaw as the commune's future.

"I go on the assumption that it will be here ten or twenty years from now. At least I've made the emotional commitment for that. But I can't see things that far ahead. I dig the people here enough to see them as an indefinite family that would continue. As for numbers, I don't know. We might grow by three, four, or five people. If we stay in a city area, you have a size problem. But we're thinking about a semirural area and commuting into a city. It's conceivable that Laura will want to live with a man, and that they'll be welcomed into the commune, if that's what they want."

Did Hibbie feel as much married to the commune itself as to Peter, her husband?

"Not at this point. Breaking down the couple units is very slow. I'd like to break them down to the extent where we had very close relations, including sexual ones, with different people. I still see my primary relationship with Peter, but without being threatened by other relations, however strong they might become. In nearly all marriages, sex is mostly possession, today we're at a point of transition."

I asked Hibbie to describe some of the best moments she had experienced in the commune, and also some of the worst.

"The good moments and the destructive moments are usually the same," she responded. "One person has to burst out with a feeling about another, or about the whole community. It's a moment charged with love, or hostility, or both, and it takes several hours to work it out, but it brings us together in new and strong ways.

"We have to face anybody's personal crisis immediately—when someone is really opening himself for some kind of reassurance. That gets to the whole idea of the commune. No matter how late it is, or how tired you might be, it really has to be done."

How did Hibbie view Hibbie as a person?

"In high school, I was an egghead who wrote poems. I had some relationships with people but wasn't really in love. I was much more into expression, identity, and a lot of that stuff. I'd be reading all the time—trying to figure things out. I'm not a group person at all; I hate parties. I don't like to go and sit around and talk. I'm an artist, so a good deal of energy goes into working by myself. I get a lot of satisfaction out of that very alone kind of working and what it can produce. As an adult, I've always had very close relationships with both women and men. I've always been in love or living with somebody."

Hibbie thought of the people in the commune as individuals and believed she had a very personal relationship with each of them. "I relate to persons here in twos and threes, unless we're having an intense kind of thing with all of us together. But the best conversations are usually with just one other person. We've got so much to learn from each other; it's part of our continual growth.

"It's threatening, however; after all, we were brought up to see our identity as an adult in the nuclear family. Now we've come to recognize that, no matter how much you love someone, one person isn't enough for an adult to share all facets of life with—and it's a bit scary."

Did Hibbie love everyone in the commune?

"Yes, defining love as a generalized kind of warmth. But that doesn't mean I can always talk to them. There's no one here whom I don't want to get to know better—there's a couple I really don't know well at all, and two or three I feel completely committed to. Some of the differences come out of practical realities—like, Peter and Jen are home most, take care of John most, and have an opportunity to get to know each other. And Amanda and I are very interested in women's liberation, so this brings us together. But relating to each other isn't a problem of setting aside a time for it, or anything like that; it just happens.

"I can't conceive of a time when everyone loved everybody equally, but we don't feel we have to. On the whole, we're pretty comfortable with each other. I don't feel the need for superficial chit-chat. Of course, when someone comes in from work, there may be small talk about how it went today. And there are lots of relaxed moments, just being in a room together, not making any effort to deepen a friendship."

Hibbie was working in a day-care center in order to earn needed money, but hoped, after six or eight months, to be able to devote full time to her art work. The desire for a child was also strong. "All of us have been talking about adopting kids," she said. "We've been thinking about a black kid. We probably won't, though; we're all pretty political and adoption could be a way of being patronizing to black people."

Jen and I talked in the room upstairs she shared with Chuck. As with everyone in the commune, they kept surprisingly few personal possessions around. Jen, holding her baby, John, sat on the bed; on the wall behind her was a Modigliani painting of a woman. Jen closely resembled the woman in face-structure, coloring, and a sense of vulnerability in her eyes, and the smiles of both held mixed meanings. Her hair was tightly drawn back on her head and tied in back; Jen was wearing a white sweater with yellow and blue flowered slacks. Like most of the others, she went barefoot inside the house.

"If everybody in the commune decided to stay together in a lifetime commitment," she told me, "we'd probably want to take the same last name. We're already decided that all the children will have the same middle name."

The process which led her to the commune was by now familiar.

"Chuck and myself had both grown up in the typical middle-class thing; after three years of marriage, we found ourselves dissatisfied. I was working in a child-welfare place and Chuck was teaching and getting his master's degree. We had a lot of money, a nice apartment, and we were terribly bored.

"When we moved here and entered the co-op, we had some financial difficulties, but it was then we began to know each other as people. We also met Amanda and Willie in the co-op. It was a step toward communal living because you had to make decisions as a house. You learn to deal with conflict and you get over the hangups about possessions. We brought to the co-op a refrigerator that we gave to the house. But we had those hangups about 'It's mine, I'm just lending it to the house.' It was a matter of giving ourselves to the house, too. You had to give up your privacy to some extent. For example, people had to go through our apartment to the storeroom. That bothered me for the first year. Afterward, I thought, 'So what?' People were always in our apartment. We would go to bed and the guys would go on watching TV in the living room.

"When the guys came down to watch TV, they'd go into the refrigerator for snacks, and this used to annoy me. It finally dawned on me that it's much more important to have friends who could feel free to go to our refrigerator. Then, there were times when the guys went out and bought food and put it in the refrigerator. Food became a very reciprocal thing. All this helped prepare me so that the decision to enter the commune just seemed very natural."

Jen played with John on the bed as she described her life in the commune.

"There have been times here, when there were a lot of guests, that we wanted to be alone for a while. We can always go to our rooms, of course. Once, though, it got to a point where I wanted to sit in the living room and put on a certain record and listen to it without asking anyone.

"This is an extremely busy house. There are so many things going on at the same time. My parents came for a weekend to take their first look at John, their first grandchild. They were here during the day, but I think they were glad to stay at a motel at night; it was pretty exhausting for them."

I asked Jen about the danger of the commune turning in on itself, becoming too self-absorbed. "Most of us have too many friends outside that we groove on," she insisted. "It would be a real down to live in a place where you couldn't have people over. Besides, we have lots of mutual friends. Of course, there's a war of personalities always going on; I wouldn't have it any other way. We've got similar opinions about lots of things, but you couldn't say we always agree. The good part is that when you have a conflict, you deal with it. If you're really pissed about something, you bring it out. Chuck and I need more practice on this. The middle-class thing is to feel guilty about the feelings you have, keeping them to yourself until you blow up at someone."

I asked her to give me an example.

"A couple of weeks ago, I felt people weren't paying enough attention to John. If he was a commune baby, people should not just feed him but love him. Instead of saying 'Hey, why don't you hold him after you feed him?' it got to the point where I was hostile. But now I say, 'When you feed him, don't hold him flat on his back,' without feeling guilty about it. And people have told me things about how to handle him. I have a tendency, as soon as he whimpers, to pick him up. This is natural for a mother with her first child. Several people have said it's good for him to cry and wake up a little before you feed him; that way he won't fall asleep. If you learn something and don't share it, what's the good of it?

"It's the same in the operation of the house. If I'm going to throw out leftovers, I'll mention it to somebody else who's around. Phone calls too. Either I'll tell somebody else there was a message, or I'll write it down. This is important about keeping lists, too. Unless you write it down, somebody going shopping won't know."

What did the commune do about money?

"We have a petty cash thing. That's normally used for grocery shopping or miscellaneous stuff. Then, we have a bank account which we all contribute to. Each of us pays a specific share. It's not exactly according to income but that's what we're aiming at.

"Eventually we hope to work it out so that whoever gets a paycheck, we just put it all into one account. And if I need clothes, or medical insurance or car insurance, it would all come out of one fund. That way, we would be supporting each other. We've thought that in the future maybe two or three of us might work for a while—even in something we didn't like—and then we'd take off and do the thing we'd really like and let others take their turns supporting us."

Jen conceded that she was still absorbed in finding an

identity. "In some ways, I still define myself in terms of other people's images of me. But during my pregnancy, I really learned something when it hit me that I wasn't conforming in any sense to my mother's image of me. We went to a hospital and there was a really fine doctor there. He asked me if I were particularly anxious about something. I got hysterical. He said, 'Your mother is getting to you, isn't she?' I had always worried about pleasing her, and how then she might approve of me, but she never did."

Jen's parents were Jews who had to flee for their lives from Nazi Germany. "I was raised in a family in a liberal Jewish environment," she explained. "I kind of grew up in the temple. As a teenager, I reacted strongly. My mother called me a Jewish anti-Semite because I wouldn't go out with Jewish boys. Actually, the Judeo-Christian tradition has served to maintain a lot of evil values in our society. Racism is easily justified by people who say, 'Black people are that way because they don't go out and work.' Not long ago, I had a tremendous argument with my father about James Forman's 'Black Manifesto.' He called it blackmail and related it to what Hitler did in Nazi Germany; for him, it simply conjured up a picture of violence.

"He's a typical liberal: 'If you can change people's attitudes, and if black people will only cooperate with whites who are trying to advance them, then. . . .' This is racist because it implies black people can't help themselves. The civil-rights movement turned out to be something for white liberals to do in order to get rid of their guilt. I don't think if you changed the attitude of every white person in this country toward blacks, anything would be changed; institutional control is something more than a conglomeration of attitudes.

"When I was in high school, I was into the beatnik thing. Maybe it was a middle-class rebellion. We'd buy long dangling earrings; at sixteen, I had my ears pierced. I dressed a little crazier than anybody else and never went out with guys my parents liked. But I never considered myself a hippie. You know, the whole thing of dropping out because society is so degenerate, and you have to look different from everybody else."

Jen didn't look very different now, as she sat across from me. In fact, she looked like thousands of other young women, casually dressed, strongly motivated by a desire to tear down false images.

"Chuck used to have a full beard and much longer hair than he does now. We didn't think we were particularly hippie looking until we had such trouble finding a house—nobody would even let us look. And when they found it was three couples who were married, they didn't want to touch us with a ten-foot pole. I always considered myself as looking straight. Yet straight people define me as hippie when they just see me."

Jen considered her college experience fairly typical. "I did well in school, and I knew where I was going. From the age of sixteen, I was going to be a social worker. And I knew I'd get married.

"I went with a guy for two and a half years in college. There were things about me I couldn't let him know, and there were things about him he couldn't let me know, and occasionally they just slipped out. He had real problems about sex, his own desires and needs; he's been brought up as a strict Catholic. I feel I had real problems about sex, too, despite a liberal family. My brother had a lot of premarital sex, but I never slept with anybody until I met Chuck. And my family assumed I hadn't.

"I had a college roommate for four years. We were like sisters. Although our personalities were different, I don't think I hid any part of myself from her, nor she from me. But now she's living the suburban thing—a fifty-thousand-dollar home, and in a few years maybe something fancier. I've wanted either to give up writing to her altogether or else say something important. I wanted to write about politics, but couldn't. Finally, I told her how disappointed I was, that all we seemed able to communicate was news. I tried to explain my deep concern about women's liberation. She wrote back that she doesn't feel oppressed at all. At least she talked to me, after all those years! I'm going to write back about how I feel about her views; now I won't be worried about being polite."

To Jen, women in America are oppressed. "Yes," she insisted, "*I'm* oppressed in terms of what society has defined for me as feminine, and what I should be in order to be a woman. It's no accident, for example, that I went into social work. It's a nice thing for a middle-class Jewish girl from the East to want to be. Or a teacher. But women don't have the stamina or intelligence, we've been made to understand, for law school or med school.

"What an American woman should want to be, we're taught, is just a wife and mother. In the nuclear family, this makes her essentially a slave, and the best consumer American capitalism can find. She's a showpiece for her husband—if she's pretty; therefore, a woman always has to be pretty. One of the most liberating things I've ever done is to stop wearing eye makeup.

"Here in the commune, men and women cook, clean, wash the dishes, mow the lawn, and build things. The women all want to take a course in car mechanics because we're sick of being exploited by car garages. Some of us want to take karate."

Jen and I had our talk in midmorning, when the house was deserted except for John. I asked how she felt about his being a commune baby.

"When he was born, we talked about that," she said. "Willie claimed he didn't want to be a father in any sense or take any responsibility for John. Amanda never made her position clear. I was disappointed. For a while, I didn't know if we could ask Willie to do anything for John, but it's worked out. Now everybody wants John to be a commune child, and Willie is learning to help.

"We all feel John doesn't belong just to Chuck and me, simply because he's ours biologically. The others have the right to raise him, just as much as we do. Of course, some people have more to do with him than others. The main thing is that we're trying to find alternatives in lifestyle. We're fighting the idea that a child is a possession, like a TV set or a car; if he does something the mother and father don't like, they feel they've failed. That's a very subtle thing for most parents, but it makes a difference in how they relate to a kid."

I asked Jen what Chuck was going to do about working or returning to school.

"Chuck may eventually get his Ph. D. Now he feels depressed because he thinks he failed. He's been going to school for eight years, defining himself by the fact that he was going to be a professional sociologist. For the moment, he's thinking about who he is—a member of this commune, a husband (I hesitate to use the word because of what it implies; I'd rather say, a person who relates to me on a very intimate basis), someone who cares for John. This is more important to him right now than becoming a professional sociologist, or some kind of status-success."

Jen looked out the window, and returned to the question of her own identity.

"I'm not just Chuck's wife," she said firmly. "I'm not just a social worker. I've spent seven years going to school to be a professional social worker, and now that I'm finished, I'm not sure it's what I want to be. *It's* a fucked up role too, doing society's dirty work for them—working with unwed mothers, getting them ready to conform to society's expectations of them."

Despite her criticism of existing institutions, Jen still professed guarded optimism about the possibility of social change in America.

"I don't think our generation will create any great breakthrough. But revolution begins at home. If we can raise our kids with new values, we can be a part of something important. I don't know; maybe nothing will happen; we may just be coopted. In some ways, we already are. For example, in the commune we own three very expensive stereos and thousands of dollars worth of books and records. Economically, we're living no differently than many other middle-class people. We're living in a physical style we're accustomed to.

"We've all gone through the self-flagellation. It's inevitable, because we're members of a group that oppresses others. Despite the fact we're doing something for possible social change, I don't think the guilt will ever go away. It's not personal guilt, but look what America has done in Vietnam, to Latin America, to blacks, to the American Indian."

I asked Jen what "love" meant to her.

"When John was born four weeks ago, when they cleared the stuff off from his eyes and ears, and they held him up, I thought, 'What a funny looking little creature.' If they had shown me all the babies they had in the nursery, it would have taken me a while to identify him. It's only been in the last two weeks that I've developed a special sense of him. I like to be near him and hold him. I don't necessarily mean that he belongs to me, that he's my child. He's the commune's child. If the commune broke up, it would be like a divorce, and kids in it would suffer just like in a divorce.

"My love for Chuck? I can honestly say that I love everyone in the commune. Of course, it's not the same kind of thing I feel for Chuck, because, if the commune broke up, most likely Chuck and I would stay together."

What did it mean for Jen to be "married" to everybody in the commune?

"Intellectually, I know what that means. Emotionally, I'm not sure. What does it mean to relate to the word 'marriage' only on a sexual level? I don't think anyone in this commune has a need to relate sexually to any one other than a marriage partner. But if the commune broke up, I'd feel like a man and a woman who get divorced and break up the family.

"I feel toward the people in the commune much as I did toward Chuck in the first year of our marriage. We really didn't know each other very well, despite the fact that we'd gone together. It's strange not to really know someone you've been married to for three and a half years. But in the past half year, we're growing with each other.

"In the coop, Chuck and I started talking to other people on a deep level, about how we felt psychologically prepared for communal living. And that set us off talking seriously to each other. I became aware of feelings Chuck had that I'd never known about. It was really strange. Well, now this same sort of thing is beginning to happen with other people in the commune."

Jen laughed and explained a current problem which called attention to their group identity. "We can't get a bank account in all of our names, unless we incorporate," she said. "It's kind of a freaky issue: us and the state, the state and us."

Laura is the sole unmarried member of the commune. She is good to be around—friendly, attractive, interested in other people, her intensity nicely contained in an easy, natural charm. When speaking, she has a tendency to start a sentence, stop, seem to shift to a new track, then start out again; but, if one is attentive, he will notice that all this is only a different way of focusing on the original idea.

"I was always aware I was a single girl among these married people," Laura told me. "The feeling I was riding on is that I wanted to live with *these* people. It's almost a coincidence that they're married and I'm not."

She paused and looked down at the floor for a moment, a mannerism she repeated several times during our interview.

"My being here," she went on, "almost makes it an issue whether the couple is the essential unit, or the individual is. We're related to each other as people. The sex makes a difference primarily to the people who are together as couples."

What, if anything, aside from the obvious, did Laura see as the difference between men and women?

"In your everyday life, as you experience people, the sex thing is—well, that isn't the road I wanted to start it on.

The difference between men and women seems to be a social statement rather than a psychological or physiological statement. The institution that fits into this is the family, the unit of economic exploitation.

"On more of a personal level, as you experience people, sex doesn't really seem to be the difference. That's why we can act primarily as human beings instead of sex symbols. Our differences seem to be very interchangeable. The stereotypes are so wrong. We don't want to judge people as social categories. No roles. People."

Laura was convinced that she had found the same sense of security as the married people in the commune. "People remain insecure in coupling; but, of course, there's a kind of trust that's added. My being able to live here shows that my comfort doesn't depend on some role or false definition of security. Not that I don't have my own sadness. Naturally, I've thought sometimes, I've no one to go to my room with. But I can't get too uptight about that or I'll be unhappy. This is a place where I can have a security and don't have to be married to get it. Marriage isn't the only institution where people can relate and come together."

She saw no threat to her individuality in this adopted lifestyle.

"I don't fit my judgments into a mold. We just happen to share a lot of common feelings. Communes have never been what they are now. We're breaking out of another social unit and into this—*creating* it.

"Take McLuhan's idea of the global village. We're part of a social revolution—today's youth have had so much experience by the time they're twenty. We're all in our twenties, and we meet sixteen-year-olds who have already had the same experiences—it's blowing their minds. And all the while TV is bringing information about the whole world into your house."

I asked Laura about her childhood; she looked at me and smiled.

"I was twenty-three yesterday," she said.

"I lived in a large suburb for eighteen years and I didn't like it. My parents have since moved, and I've lost all reason ever to go back. I wasn't unhappy; I had a good home. My nuclear family, as a unit that existed, was pretty good. I had two brothers. The whole thing doesn't fit either my textbook or soap-opera description of a family.

"But there was sensory deprivation, living in that neighborhood. People weren't really free; there was a lot of social lobotomizing going on."

She looked down at the floor again, and when she resumed speaking, the subject had become more general. "It's difficult to be a person; you play so many roles. It's not easy to break out of the husband and wife syndrome, and it's not in people's genes. There's a lot more freedom in people's psychobiology than they realize. Being isolated from themselves is a kind of schizophrenia. Insecurity is a part of being human. People are separate in their lives; they're alone and they can perish from it. I've experienced it. I've experienced all this, but when I look at different people, I see it in them, too."

Laura tried to explain the process which led her to come into the commune.

"I had gone away to college for some reason that didn't exist. When I got there, I found out that there were some people I liked, but I was still being motivated by reasons that weren't very sound.

"You look at the texture of everyday middle-class existence, and you realize this is not the good life. The good life is being happy, liking who you are, who you're with, what you're doing. It's being able to think about your life and almost wanting to sing about it. That's my whole idea now. I'm not preparing to live my life, I'm living it. So I'm concerned about what other people's lives are like, because my life is never an isolated thing.

"During my senior year as an undergraduate, I lived in a freaky house, filled with unusual people. We all knew each other, but somehow we were very separate—it wasn't a commune. We had really come together by accident. Anyway, this gave me a dissatisfaction with living unhappily—separately —the way I might have had to if I'd never broken out.

"A lot of people now—mostly young—want to break down the old patterns. You wake up and see yourself doing things you don't want to be doing. Values change—white gets turned into black, and you learn something. I believe in some kind of evolution of psychic abilities. There's territory being broken into, in terms of explorations of inner space."

Could drugs play any part in this?

"I'm pro-drugs," Laura said, "as a weapon. They're a means of liberation. They take you places you've never been. I wonder about their use—your head has to be in a certain place. But I still wonder about kids using them; yet that's the basic mistake—telling other people how to live their lives. It's going to be complicated for a while, if you're sixteen or seventeen, taking drugs. But there's nothing that can be done to stop it. Kids are getting arrogant, with their combination of purity and confidence and strength. And somehow, children are growing up without feeling guilty."

Laura had been confirmed as an Episcopalian but was not interested in what was usually called religion. "My oldest brother," she recalled, "went through confirmation classes when he was twelve, but when he was given the right to make a decision about going through with it, he stopped immediately. I toyed around with it for a while and finally decided to be confirmed. But when a boy asked me, on the steps of our high school, 'Do you believe in God?', I had to say no. As for religious insights, I can take some interest—explore—share. Religion isn't an institution or set of practices or body of knowledge; it's more an experience. It's when they start writing things down that they really get themselves in trouble. They quote things to which they can be tied."

Laura had very definite views about the need for social change but found it difficult as a student to get beyond her own life and do anything that would help others. "I'm going to school now even though it's not the best way for me to be doing what I want to do, but there's no alternative. What America is doing to the rest of the world is terrible, and all the while I'm wasting time with all the garbage that goes with the university. No wonder the kids talk about violence. And the riots in the ghettos, how can I take a stand against that? Still, somewhere along the line, you've got to learn to stop rioting. Spontaneous acts of *refusal* make more sense. Like refusing to be a colonialist."

I mentioned the feeling of some students that repression in America was on the rise, and that they might end up in jail. "I don't think it's imminent," she said. "But it's hard to believe in alternatives; I've even considered leaving the country. Reaction is gaining and they've got the guns; I could be put in prison without committing any act of violence myself. Still, we've got the kids with us; that's why I think—hope—something may have really changed.

"What was best about life in the commune was that it was a living, growing thing. Each day we change. I was in a cocoon for awhile. Now I can see myself developing everyday, almost like a child. Of course, there's a lot of pain involved in the growing. But my bad moments are more concerned with doubts about myself than the commune.

"Last year was intolerable, before we began living together. I wondered about the world—you know, *how people can live*. Just before we started the commune, I wrote a letter, speculating as to what it would be like—I said we'd all have to be in love.

"Part of the idea is that the commune will help us to be secure in everyday life. We think we're living better than we could any other way. Money makes a lot of things possible, but it also isolates. Here we're working toward socialism in the commune, economically. And we've broken down a lot of privacies. People are responsible for other people in a lot of different ways. We realize that just living together in a house doesn't make us a commune."

As for marriage, it mostly meant permanency and solidarity. "The trouble is," Laura conceded, "I don't like to think in terms of, say, from *this* point to the *end* of my life. I don't look backward to a past and forward to a future; marriage is what joins these things together. Marriage is a coupling, a real binding that has no time dimension. But it can't prevent people splitting up. People change. We all know that."

Laura looked down at her hands again, then directly into my face.

"We're all aware people here have different languages. Since there are many tongues, there is some misunderstanding of the different languages. Instead of speaking of levels—coming up, or down, to someone else's—I hope we can all together go to a *different* level."

Peter is the only member of the commune who wears a radical look. This is due in part to his disheveled hair, in part to his eyes, which can appear to be very angry or suddenly laughing. He seems, in the beginning, the hardest person in the commune to get *at*. Even his speech bolsters this impression—labyrinthine, frequently academic, but also highly creative and personal. Once preliminary barriers are overcome, however, Peter is extremely open, and one of the friendliest people in the commune. He is married to Hibbie.

"If you're going to change society," Peter began, "you have to change the way human beings look at, and relate to, each other. A commune is a means of getting away from ranking people all the time. I don't mean something anarchistic; it's just that there can be order based on nonranking."

But might not the commune, I suggested, be too self-absorbed to be involved in political action?

"We've worried about too much navel-gazing and not being able to do something with the society. That would be a copout. So we decided the commune should, in theory, be a base for external political action. But there are practical difficulties: we've just gone through a summer that's been discouraging for me politically; there's a baby in the commune; fall means going back to school, and for me, entering graduate school; dogs are running around the house; and I find I'm not all that interested in politics. I realize our fears of withdrawing were very valid—it's an easy thing to do."

Peter, at twenty-two, is the youngest member of the commune. He attended college for two years in the Midwest before coming to California with his wife.

"I've always been very active politically, not as much in civil rights as ban the bomb. I was a very big politico on my campus and even got asked by the president to leave. I met Hibbie there while we were undergraduates.

"I've always been very close to somebody, it seems to me. Even my big brother. When he went away to college, I was in the eighth grade. I've always had a tendency to know one person very well. When I was a sophomore in high school, I didn't have a close friend and it was a disturbing year. In college, there were about ten of us, very close, trying to fight the administration."

Peter grew up in a suburb of New York City; his parents were nonpracticing Jews. "My mother," he explained, "is into this thing about Jewish culture—it has a great heritage, she said. But the gene flow of ancestors for ten generations doesn't connect me. From one point of view, Nazi Germany is part of my heritage, too.

"I remember, when I was five, my brother who was nine was telling me to pray. I ended with 'goddamn it' just to irritate him because prayer or God made no sense to me.

"Religion never meant anything to me. Infinity in space means space never began—no creator. There's no 'correct' up there. Take the case of the Nazi who thinks he is right. He's about to kill somebody and I say 'I'm right from my point of view.' And I stop him. I don't believe in *a* right but what I *find* is right.

"There's no objective basis for any morality or ethics, whatever they are. Man is a thinking being; that's what means the most to me. So man can go on to conquer those things that challenge him, and have physical and metaphysical pleasure. That is what is right for man, for me; but it has no objective basis; it's right for me and my life."

Like the others, Peter saw ominous signs in contemporary American society.

"My roots are American, but I don't know if I can be really productive here," he said. "If this country goes through a lot of convulsions, it would be very hard to keep going with the commune. We'd like a semirural area, where there are a number of community colleges within fifty miles, with maybe three out of seven people pulling in regular salaries—then we could live simply. But this society can get to the point where seven people can't even live together safely. So we may not be able to stay together.

"People our age have a tendency to say the country is turning fascist. Maybe it's just staying much the same, and we may end up with the same kind of government we've had right along—Vietnam may be 'solved,' as was the Congo situation, and be a continual mess."

What about the possibility of revolution in America?

"You can't make a revolution in a counterrevolutionary age," he said bleakly. "In some way, we're wrapping ourselves up and waiting for another generation. In terms of protest, it's a pessimistic picture, but that's what I feel tonight. I just had a long talk with a professor friend, about how some people are saying the most important question is whether you can, as a revolutionary, kill a pig. A cop. That's not where I'm at right now. Right now, my political head is unscrewed, to the point where it's best to leave it alone. I don't want to screw it on. I want it to be screwed on.

"Somebody says, 'All these people are dying. I want to find a way to help.' I will hear that again and react. But my reaction will not be an emotional one—a guilt reaction. I want sound pragmatic politics that may be anti-utopian—where I might get dirty hands, hopefully from doing what is right in terms of the society versus the individual.

"Sometimes it's important to have a strong social-political

organization where people are not just doing their thing. I've always thought that revolutionary movements in their youth tend to be anarchistic. The Left right now is going through this—not just the Left, but all kids. It's a reaction to the order around them that's pervasively rotten; so they tend to throw out most orders. In a way, a commune is another order. We're not a hippie commune; what we're saying is, 'If I have to relate to everybody as a bastard, I'm destroyed; but there are six or seven people here I can relate to.' "

Sitting with me in the study room where we talked, Peter wore work pants and a T-shirt and was barefoot. As we got more deeply into the idea of the commune all tension had disappeared, and he seemed to come more fully alive. "You know," he said, "before we moved in, I always thought of a commune as a spoked wagon wheel. Hibbie and I knew the other people through Willie and Amanda. In the process, we got to know Chuck and Jen better. At first I was scared of a clique developing but it's kind of a blob now. If we have a discussion, it's not like taking sides. When people disagree, the variations tend to spread themselves around. Person 'X' might tend to get aggressive on one topic, but not on another. Of course, everyone has his own eccentricities; something is bound to come up when you're odd man out. But the way we live, odd man eventually becomes everybody. At the same time, some people tend to get dumped on more than others, and some are more flexible than others."

I returned to my question about feeling married to all the people in the commune. "Potentially, it's that way," Peter said thoughtfully. "I tell myself that it's still an experiment, a transition, but hell, everything's a transition. I have to admit that if I knew my wife as little as I know some of the people in the commune, I wouldn't have married her yet.

"My marriage has been very intense; we really knew everything about each other before we got married. Even now we have a tendency to leave the others for an hour during the day and just talk. I wouldn't say I was married to everybody until I felt that intensely about them and enough things had come into the open. I know I'll feel that way about some of them, but I'm not sure who. I'm trying not to say things before I believe them. It would mean a real, intense relationship with people, where I'm as close to them as I am to my wife, where there's nothing we wouldn't talk about, living together with this constant sense of each other. But the coupleness of the commune will be broken down. Within a couple of years I'll get to know the others almost as well as I know my wife."

Peter resisted the idea of the commune as a witness within society, pointing toward an alternative style of life. "I'm not really into morality," he said, scowling. "You know, 'This is my stance vis-à-vis the world, so I don't have to compromise.' In one way, I feel somewhat more selfish about it. The things I don't compromise on are sometimes contradictory. The commune is more of a social act than an individual act; I'm not sure what a social witness would be.

"I'm seeing if people can relate to each other this way in social organization, as a sociologist. But I don't want to make it academic—it's real life. In fact, I'm not sure I want to be a professional in academic life. At one time I wanted to be a professor in a relatively small college and put out important books that would mean things to people. I don't feel that way anymore; I don't see my life fitting into this society. All I can say now is that I'm in graduate school this year; I can't see anything beyond that at this point."

He was confident he could avoid military service, possibly because of physical disability, perhaps as a hardship case. "If the chips were down," he admitted, "I don't want to leave the country or go to jail, but I would rather leave. Turning in my draft card is a political act I want to participate in; it saddens me that guys are doing bad things to their lives because of it. There's only one person I know who seems to have come through jail as a whole person. I want to overturn an entire system but don't think you can do it by fighting the draft."

Since we were sitting in the study, surrounded by the

commune library, neatly divided into categories, Peter thought of a practical test of group living, related to his own study habits: "I tend to carry on a conversation with an author in the margins of any book," he told me. "This poses questions for us, however, so I ask permission of the commune to write in a book. To take notes on sheets of paper instead, is difficult for me."

Maintaining the library also required a common effort.

"If I'm taking a course where it's vital to use a particular book, and somebody has loaned it out without asking me, it's a bad scene," he said. "If I'm going to loan a book to somebody, I try to ask people, 'Does anybody need this?' "

Peter and I walked downstairs to the basement in order to let the dogs out into the backyard.

"This house is built around the theory that if somebody is bugged by noise, there's someplace to go to be alone. If someone is typing in the study, others can always use the basement here." He showed me around, pointing out the accomplishments of group cooperation. "It used to smell bad," Peter said. "We cleaned it up, and we strung ropes and curtains to make guest quarters." I admired the new shelving which pleased him. "I've always wanted to do stuff like carpentry," he admitted. "And the basement is a good party place for, say, a dozen people."

I asked for more details of adjustments to group living.

"Willie and Amanda play a stereo late at night when they're going to sleep. It has to be soft because we can hear it. Hibbie and I run on an entirely different schedule; we go to bed earlier and get up earlier. As of now, I think there's a cooking schedule. We want to know the day before what to expect. Laura came home today at four-thirty and said she'd cook. I felt this was a bit ad hoc; what if everybody came home late? It's still an issue because we are working it out. He showed me an open memorandum to everybody signed by Chuck and smiled as I read aloud: "Could someone please buy stamps today? And could we maybe have a left-over supper to use up all that stuff in the refrigerator?"

Peter passed quickly over money problems, but admitted that discussion of "special needs" tended to come up at the end of each month. He was amused by the common learning process caused by the presence of John, the commune baby. "It's a funny scene. Not all of us are equally into the baby. It's mostly Jen, Hibbie, and I, in that order. Feeding the baby at night is hard for Chuck because he's working. So every other night I get up at three, and hope to get back to bed at four-fifteen."

I asked Peter about drugs in the commune. "We've all been through stages when drugs have been more important to us than they are now," he explained. "We're pretty negative about people who are stoned all the time or use it for a social crutch, but I like going to the movies stoned. Some of us have never really been into drugs; none of us is ignorant. We started five or six years ago before the real explosion. I feel it is a stupid thing to get busted for."

We walked back upstairs from the basement and were silent for a moment. Peter frowned, then relaxed with a gesture of total acceptance. "You know," he said, "I wanted to be a part of the glorious revolution that was coming. Now I don't see it coming so fast. Nor do I know what to do in order to make it come. Though it should definitely come.

"At the same time," he continued, "I profess to be very happy. In an odd sense, I feel very strongly the recognition of ambiguities is an important way for me to put something together."

Willie is tall—the tallest person in the commune—a strong, bearded figure usually attired in khaki pants and a T-shirt, and has a bag of books slung over his shoulder. In conversation, Willie gets so directly to the point that at first his style can be misconstrued as abrasive. Talking with him a little longer, one is impressed by an extraordinary stable human being who insists on mutual openness, with a powerful drive for understanding. He cuts through sham instantly. Willie is twenty-two and married to Amanda; the accent of his native New York City is still discernible.

"There are all sorts of different communes," Willie told me. "From what I've been able to gather, ours is one of the less dramatic ones. We'd be described by many people on the outside world as reasonably serious, sort of older, less hippie. We're not heavily into drugs. We're not here just to say we're free and can do anything we want. But, we do share a lot with other communes, in the sense that it's a political action just to try to restructure your life in ways that haven't been provided socially."

Willie and I were talking in the study. It was earlier in the morning than either of us usually liked to be engaged in a serious conversation, and we were still nursing our instant coffee.

I asked Willie about the possibility of the commune taking group action.

He shook his head. "We're not an action group in the usual political sense. Communes are really examples of self-control—having some say in your own life."

Didn't that mean political withdrawal, I pursued. "It's hard to judge, though, because none of us has an absolute commitment to a political level we can judge by. I don't think we'll end up withdrawing because the group itself helps us become aware of what is going on both inside and outside. Anyway, I'm not certain of the value of most political activities, whether in fact they deal with issues the way they need to be dealt with.

"Besides Vietnam and racism, another concern for us, of course, is male chauvinism and women's liberation. So we're always engaging in some type of political thinking. If you think that you're part of an essentially racist-imperialist society, it's important to try to build a life in which you can disassociate yourself at least from certain aspects of it. Like oppression of women or of black people. So we try to do this, not just with rhetoric, but with the way we live."

I asked Willie if he thought there were differences between men and women.

"Probably, yes," he said, "but they're created by society. They're probably not biologically innate. Women are people and men are people. But society holds that a man is what he does and how he reacts. The same with women. Our culture has engineered role concepts that are dehumanizing for both parties, especially women. Men have a better deal of it, for we have women to take care of our house and all the things related to it.

"For all practical purposes, individual people are different. Maybe women are somewhat different from men, but that's not the issue. Whether or not biological differences exist, they're overridden by the way people are socially created. Women are supposedly happy taking care of a home. But if they hadn't learned to be housewives, they'd spend their whole lives doing the same jobs and being unhappy about it.

"In a way, acting out women's liberation is the single most important aspect of the way we're trying to live. It's also part of trying to form positive identities of who we are, independent of how society identifies us: as orange or black, what you *do*, how much money you have, a man or a woman. To say that we're liberating ourselves may be a little melodramatic but in a real sense it's true. Of course, no single group of people can really be liberated without everybody—the whole society—moving in that direction."

I asked Willie about the possibility of the commune principle being "coopted" by the society outside it.

A tired expression came into his eyes for a moment. "We're very much aware of that danger," he answered. "The likelihood of this occurring at various stages, and how the meaning of various things we're trying to do may be changed. We don't have any criteria of moral purity. There's bound to be a tension between realistic political action and really living decently. In a way they're contradictory, although that's what we're looking for in the commune."

Willie got up to make more coffee.

"Political action requires self-abnegation and discipline," he continued. "The media are great levelers; they talk about things that are happening but drain them of meaning. Words are rather helpless before the media. We heard a TV ad that said 'Join the money-making revolution—become a money-making revolutionary.' I worry about *Look* and *Life* doing articles on communes; maybe it's important but it's dangerous."

He stretched his legs out, recalling misconceptions he had encountered, even among his sociology students.

"I was talking in a class about living communally, there were some amazing discussions, like about economics. I would say, 'Six people can have a vacuum cleaner instead of every two. It's cheaper and easier, and you learn to share things, which means relationships with other people.' The kids would say, 'Suppose you all wanted to use the vacuum cleaner at the same time.' It was a turnoff, a way of not looking at the real issues. Maybe if they thought about it again, they'd realize how foolish this was."

I asked Willie to explain some of the factors that led to the commune getting started.

"People have a vested interest in their own life situation," he said; "that's what makes it livable. People like my parents have to justify their own way to themselves. It's not a lifestyle I would be able to justify now, but I can't condemn it—I didn't face the things they faced, and they're older than I. But it's sad to see eighteen-year-old kids justify the way they're going to live in thirty years. Yes, having a vacuum cleaner for two people.

"We tried to start from what seemed most reasonable—basically, my criterion is ecological. I know that psychologically one of the worst things anybody can do is take himself too seriously, but people are really facing serious problems. When I get pessimistic, like thinking about chemical-biological warfare, it pisses me off that we're going to destroy the rest of the world and not just ourselves."

Willie had told his parents about financial arrangements

in the commune and been disappointed by their reaction. "They've worried about my getting cheated, and all the things progressives should know better about," he said. "Fact is, I've always been sort of uptight about money, because of how I grew up. I'm still not entirely willing to throw all my money into the commune. Right now, we have a modified plan that gives the commune all it needs and still doesn't take everything from everybody."

Although he liked the idea of always having people he liked around, Willie conceded that there was sometimes a problem of privacy.

"We used to invite friends over to dinner a lot. Now we bump into each other in the kitchen and joke about not having friends to dinner—they're already here. Still, I don't always feel so free in terms of time and space, mostly space. Not being able to get off alone, or alone with people." He paused, and corrected himself. "But that's not really true. Even when there are too many people, it's better than not having them around."

I asked Willie about the question of couples in the commune.

"Amanda and I have a feeling of a couple, but more and more we're able to refrain from sitting together, and talking as 'we.' I don't know if there will be sexual issues particularly; if they happen they happen. I don't feel any great desire for them. It might be a good thing in some ways —just being freer and looser together. But it's not automatic and could work the other way around. The important thing would be being comfortable together. It would depend on our personalities. I wouldn't push something theoretical, if people were uptight about it. But it would be nice to collaborate with each other intellectually. A bunch of good heads together—say, taking tutorials together. A few of us may sit in on an introductory Spanish class this year and then go to Mexico together next summer."

Willie stood up and walked slowly around the study.

"I have a clear picture of what's happened to me since leaving home at eighteen. Getting to know Amanda, who has the finest group of friends imaginable, and learning ego-overhaul, freed me from having to think so much about myself—what a good, funny, smart person I was—and helped me realize I had a great bunch of friends and we really liked each other, and that was enough. You know, getting out of that personal thing."

He conceded that he was still working on his involvement with John.

"I sort of take him in small doses," Willie said. "I'm not crazy about hearing him cry all the time. I'm definitely into the idea of wanting to have a child with Amanda, but that will take a few years because of school."

When he sat down again, it was to tell me that he was against organized religion.

"Religiously, my parents were nothing. They considered themselves ethnically Jewish. My grandfather's father was a rabbi in Russia. Frankly, religion is a mystifier of experience. To believe in forces that are not demonstrably operative in the world prevents you from understanding how things really work in the world. I believe in the real world, the material world. And that forces that operate in society and nature create reality and the world the way it is. Reality is socially constructed. The material world sort of creates us, and our social existence is a product of economic, historical, geographical forces.

"My idea of conscience is changing, too, from somewhere between guilt and responsibility to something different. I don't see 'good' or 'bad' people, but people as a product of a particular social situation, differently structured in conscience and intellects. It depends in part on where they're from. Laura, who grew up in the Midwest, is different from me. I'm not sure morality has an unchanging meaning. It's like a system of belief in right or wrong, or a judgment about the value of things.

"I tend to psychologize people. I might say: 'That's an immoral act, but it's a defensive act, that came from being dehumanized and not having learned to relate to people. I suppose I have a system of morality, though I don't like to call it that. But like I said, my basis for judging things is ecological. Basically, it has to do with what is good for people —dehumanizing or humanizing them, fulfilling or repressing them. This has the advantage, I think, of making my presuppositions clearer than morality does."

As for the commune's future, Willie considered himself committed. "I'm much more conscious of group divorce as a concept than group marriage. I'm determined it won't fail because of me remaining uptight or unable to be honest; but I don't feel committed in the sense that it must succeed or we must always live together. I don't expect that to happen."

I asked Willie about the commune in relation to the child he had said that he would like to have with Amanda.

He smiled, thought for a moment with his hand on his head, then leaned forward in his chair.

"Amanda and I have decided any kids we have will be raised in a commune. This eliminates having just two models for the child—the mother and father—whose fuckup is on the kid. The idea of the kid being the center of your life, this is just not a good thing.

"Kids aren't possessions, yet in America they're viewed and treated as possessions by their parents, and that's just lousy for everybody."

4

Five Vietnam Veterans

Once it was different. When we went to the District Commandant to enlist, we were a class of twenty young men, many of whom proudly shaved for the first time before going to the barracks. We had no definite plans for our future. Our thoughts of a career and occupation were as yet of too unpractical a character to furnish any scheme of life. We were still crammed full of vague ideas which gave to life, and to the war also, an ideal and almost romantic character. We were trained in the army for ten weeks and in this time more profoundly influenced than by ten years at school. We learned that a bright button is weightier than four volumes of Schopenhauer. At first astonished, then embittered, and finally indifferent, we recognized that what matters is not the mind but the boot brush, not intelligence but the system, not freedom but drill. We became soldiers with eagerness and enthusiasm, but they have done everything to knock that out of us. After three weeks it was no longer incomprehensible to us that a braided postman should have more authority over us than had formerly our parents, our teachers, and the whole gamut of culture from Plato to Goethe. With our young, awakened eyes we saw that the classical conception of the Fatherland held by our teachers resolved itself here into a renunciation of personality such as one would not ask of the meanest servant—salutes, springing to attention, parade-marches, presenting arms, right wheel, left wheel, clicking the heels, insults, and a thousand pettifogging details. We had fancied our task would be different, only to find we were to be trained for heroism as though we were circus-ponies. But we soon accustomed ourselves to it. We learned in fact that some things were necessary, but the rest merely show. Soldiers have a nose for such distinctions.

The car sped along a highway in western Pennsylvania toward an airport. A student was driving me to catch a plane after a visit to his college campus.

"Did I tell you that I was in Vietnam?" he asked suddenly. "Artillery. Just got out about four months ago."

His words were a jolt; I found myself tense and self-conscious. I couldn't help wondering if he resented me; undoubtedly he knew that I had spoken against the war at his campus. A few minutes earlier, it had seemed we were getting along famously; had I been misled by a veneer of good will? But this was foolish and unfair; I was setting up barriers, thinking in categories instead of looking at the person beside me. What *happened* to him in Vietnam, I thought—and suddenly realized, with some shame, that here was a crucial dimension of contemporary American experience to which I had never really exposed myself.

When I tuned in again, he was talking about his classes. He asked me if I'd have time for coffee at the airport before my plane, and my tension disappeared; by the time I had to get on board, we had become friends. With great simplicity, he took me into his confidence. He was living, he said, with a closeknit group of Vietnam veterans at the college, seldom venturing far outside it except for dating. He was drinking more than he had been accustomed to do. It wasn't his college courses or his occupational goals that were bothering him, and yet there was something he couldn't

Erich Maria Remarque, *All Quiet on the Western Front* (Boston, Little Brown and Company, 1929).

quite articulate, and it did have a connection with Vietnam; because of it, he felt misunderstood by, and unknown to, the rank and file of his fellow-students.

What about after college, I asked. He didn't know. He was on the point of saying something more, that neither doves nor hawks were talking about what it was really like, and I had to run. I've never seen him again, but he had taught me a lesson in humility, and made it clear that I had better get to know—and listen to—other Vietnam veterans. Since then, wherever I happened to be visiting, I would ask friends to arrange a meeting with ex-GI's whom they knew, and might want to talk about what they had been through. I had no way of knowing what their attitudes about the war might be and spared them any presentation of my opinions. What was surprising is that they seemed to be grateful for an opportunity to release long-suppressed emotions, even though the memories were often painful.

These interviews do not constitute a cross-section and offer no broad conclusions, but it is clear that for these young men involvement in the Vietnam war was the most significant event that had occurred in their lives. It had torn them out of the familiar structure of their involvement with home and school and job and girl friend, sending them far away to a foreign land where they had come face to face with hard authority and unending terror and destruction. Because of angry controversies that will probably long be associated with American involvement in Vietnam, I have given these veterans pseudonymical names and identifications—including home towns and colleges—to replace their real ones; this seemed simply an act of justice toward them, rather than inadvertently exploit their deep honesty and extreme vulnerability.

Dan Bridges is black, twenty-five years old, and holds a student personnel job at a Midwestern college. He served in Vietnam from September, 1967, to September, 1968. He has an Afro haircut and wears a neat moustache; during our interview he was wearing a gray suit with a white shirt and blue tie. "I'm clean all the time," he told me. "This is my philosophy." He also wore a conference football championship ring, which has a bright red stone, from his undergraduate days at a Big-Ten university.

"Coming back from Vietnam was a new and difficult experience," he said. "People seemed to be kind of afraid of me. They'd heard so many things about Vietnam, how it changes people. Even my family—my father's dead, but my mom and the rest of the family—didn't know what to look for.

"My first night home was a Friday, and I got into a fight at a nightclub. Social life here leaves a lot to be desired. At the time there were no nice black joints. The white places really didn't want a black person there. I went to a club that was going to charge me twenty-five dollars for a key to get in. But I felt as though, being American—I had fought for America and I was wounded twice over there—I was capable of being able to go any place I wanted. After all, I had fought in Vietnam to prove my loyalty to America. I am still under the impression that I deserve more respect now than I did before I went into the service. If somebody pushes me and simultaneously calls me 'boy'—which is what happened at the white club that first night I got back—it just doesn't settle right. The guy on the door was a big fat guy, but physically he was no problem to handle. I was in good shape and hurting."

Bridges stretched his legs, and leaned back in his chair.

"People want to know what *is* going on in Vietnam, what's happening. Well, it's a very emotional thing. I find it difficult to describe what I've been through. I can't explain even to this day.

"Two months ago, I came home from work one night. My mom was there, my two brothers, my buddy, and my sister. Out of a clear blue sky, for no apparent reason, I just began to cry. And I don't know why. I can't conclude any valid reason for this type thing. But after going through what any infantry soldier, black or white, goes through in a combat situation over there, I think he deserves a little more than is granted to him on arrival back in the United States."

What had Dan felt when he first arrived in Vietnam?

"I was scared shitless—I didn't know what to expect. Everybody there has a story to tell about Vietnam. Being a potential infantry soldier in Vietnam, you listen to them all. It seems everybody glorifies or exaggerates what's happening over there.

"For example, say that a VC [Viet Cong] guy is coming up with a rifle one hundred feet away. You just shoot him. Only by the time the story gets back to a young, gullible new G.I. over there, it's become hand-to-hand combat with the VC, you know, and after a rifle jammed."

Bridges's training took place at Ft. Jackson, South Carolina, Ft. Polk, Louisiana, and Ft. Knox, Kentucky, before he was sent to Vietnam.

"They didn't teach us much," he said. "Fundamentally, I was unprepared to go. The training period should have been longer, much more detailed, and much more to the point. The only things I knew about Vietnam were what I had read in books. All the United States Army taught us was what they wanted us to know. Everything they told us about the people and the political situation was a bullshit lie.

"I was in Vietnam for a year. I died every night. I watched my buddies die. I watched the enemy die. Why? I don't know. Here I am, a returnee from Vietnam, and I still don't know why the hell I was over there killing people, or why I allowed myself to be caught in this kind of situation."

His bitterness was so deep that I asked him if he believed that the United States should pull out of Vietnam immediately.

"It was definitely a mistake in the first place," he began, "for us to be involved in as much depth as we are in Vietnam today. We shouldn't be there but now, I think we've got to stay. I think we should fight the war as a war should be fought, winner take all, and then come right back here where we belong. I don't advocate war but I think an end with honor is the only thing. Just to pull out and come home would be bad."

He paused for a minute and smiled grimly. "The fact is,"

he said, "I find myself more patriotic than I used to be. This is a hell of a thing to say—*now* I would fight to my death anyone who would do wrongly to the United States. But that doesn't mean I'm impressed with the so-called American way of life today. I'm in love with America, the *idea* of Americanism, *not* the bullshit thing we call the United States today. America today is what it is because it was, many years ago, what it was."

Dan gestured angrily, as if to generalize about his black experience in America.

"I've been cognizant of the racial situation ever since I have been aware of me. Ever since I was old enough to understand the difference between right and wrong. That there was a thing between black and white. And it was the same thing in college, even though I was a big shot—on a football scholarship. The night before last, I was talking about it with my college roommate, who is also black. We remembered what the football coach did to the black athletes then. We wouldn't stand for it now. Like, the time the coach just grabbed a black guy by the collar and shook him, because the black athlete wouldn't say 'No, sir' and 'Yes, sir.' That coach had us all over a barrel.

"But now is a good time to be black. If I had the intelligence Einstein had, and the choice now to be black or white, I wouldn't be white. There are opportunities now to turn things around. Like, three years ago, I would have taken a back seat. Or I would have come into a place, and there would be a white girl sitting there, and I wouldn't sit next to her. Not because I was afraid of her or what she would say, but of her reaction—acting afraid, scooting over. Now I sit where I want to sit, and say 'damn you.' I'm a proud black man. Blacks are learning to identify ourselves, and it's not going to take so long."

I asked Dan what it was like to be a black G.I. in Vietnam.

"Before I went into the service I was a different guy. Altogether different. So many things happened to me in Vietnam. Like, the Vietnamese girls—the white G.I. has instilled within them the fact that the black guy is inferior. It's not anything the girls say, but you can look into their eyes and tell.

"I was in a combat unit. Thirty percent of the fighting, dying, killing G.I.'s in Vietnam are black. This isn't an official figure but it's so obvious in terms of the total number of people there and who is doing the fighting, you just have to look around. A base camp is a safe area and the safe jobs there are almost all occupied by white guys. The black soldier is sent to the front, to fight and die for this thing called America.

"All the decisions are white decisions. I was in a mechanized company as a squad leader. I had two white guys as track men; there were twelve guys on our track. You've got four platoons, and each has four squads, so you have a total of sixteen squads. Every time we'd make a combat assault, mine was always on point the first day. Or when the shit hit the fan, they'd say 'You go.' The shit got so low one time, the whole company realized the deal we were getting simply by being black. But as Americans, we're all supposed to be operating on a fair turn."

His story made me wonder what will happen when the black Vietnam veterans—thousands and thousands of them—will have finally returned to the U.S.

When I raised the question, Bridges crossed his legs, sat up straight, and thought for a moment without answering.

"There's going to be a whole lot of pissed off black G.I.'s coming home from Vietnam," Dan said finally. "And there's already a lot of pissed off Americans here. We're going to get together. The things the white man has taught us, we'll put to use.

"I'm not advocating violence in the streets. And I'm a firm believer in the Bible. The Bible says, 'You reap what you sow.' My thing is, what goes around comes around; we're all in a circle. You kick me square in the ass. I can only go around and kick you right back.

"When all is said and done, the white man has raped my

mother, killed my father, and kicks me in the ass all the time. I think that anything a black man does, and gets away clean doing something to the white man, he's justified. If five black men went downtown and robbed a bank, and got away, good!

"But it doesn't have to become as violent as a revolution. I'd hate to see anything tear down this beautiful American idea. The crazy part is, I'm in love with what America is supposed to be. I think the black man, overall, is still in love with what America is supposed to be. And I think the legitimate long-haired white man—carrying a sign, wearing a beard, wanting peace—is also in love with the same thing."

Bridges asked me if I had seen the film *Easy Rider*.

"You know," he said, "the ending really had me confused. I left the theater wondering, did the two guys kill the kids for no real motive, just for the hell of it, or out of envy because the kids did completely what they wanted to do?

"America is so fouled up now—so stereotyped and afraid. The average American seems to be afraid of anybody who thinks differently than he does. You're supposed to be able to think what you want to think. After all, one reason America is not a British colony today is that there was taxation without representation, and the colonists said, 'Bullshit. We've got a right to air our opinions.'"

Even when his words were harsh, Bridges maintained a cool manner as he spoke. His eyes, however, betrayed his anger, and a special emphasis on certain words and phrases showed when he was deeply moved.

"What will we do with the white people?" he continued. "If I could control the United States today, and had the power to destroy anyone I wanted, I wouldn't do anything to the white people—eventually they'll do it to themselves. Suddenly, they'll be on their deathbed, asking us, 'How could I have been so wrong?'

"I'm not telling you to love me. Or not to love me. I'm telling you to love God. Because, by loving God, and just believing the things that he says, you wouldn't have to do *anything.* 'Another comandment I give to you is that you love one another.'

"I have a very religious mom and I used to go to Sunday school all of the time—well, just about. It left quite an impression on me. But in an environment like a physics class, it's unusual for a person to say anything good about God. They'll ask, 'How in the world can anybody turn water into wine?' or 'How can a girl have a baby without screwing?' and stuff like this. Once in Vietnam I heard a G.I. say something about Jesus walking on the water. And the guy next to him says, 'Shit floats too,' then you wonder, how can you say anything to prove it really happened? All you can say is, 'The Bible says this and that's the only evidence I can give you.' I believe the preacher when he says, 'Jesus Christ is come down to take his chosen people up with him.' But if you see me downtown after work, drinking and raising hell, you'll probably ask yourself, 'Is this the same guy who told me this?' Of course, there's a contradiction between what I believe and what I do, but it doesn't bother me."

Bridges stood up and slowly walked around the room; there was a story he wanted to tell me but he seemed to need to be moving.

"A long time ago I had a girl who lived away out in the country with her family. There wasn't a light around their house for miles. One night I had been out there late and when I got into my father's car to drive home, I had the strongest feeling somebody or something was in the car with me. I went back into the house and got a flashlight and looked. There was nothing in the car. I started driving and I came to four miles of straight road. It was just flat and dark, and all around me there was nothing. All of a sudden, something hit me on the shoulder—just like this. And I can't explain it. And in Vietnam, the situations I was in, I should have remained in permanently—like, I should have been killed."

Bridges described the incident in detail.

"We had just come down—we'd been out walking. Our

trucks were parked on a high hill. The path was narrow and there were trees surrouding the route. We dropped all our security—just forgot about it. We were laying out, really taking it easy, and glad to be back. All of a sudden, there was a sniper. Boom! Boom! Two shots were fired and two guys were dead—the guys who were on either side of me. It's like that invisible shield you used to see on TV, a force field that wasn't going to let any harm come to me.

"Another time we were riding down the trail; when we stopped, guys were sitting down on top of the tracks. One guy got a direct hit with a B 40 rocket. He was spliced all over everybody—there'd be part of his intestines on your tongue. You had to wipe it off, as well as all his blood on your clothes and face. If it had been a few seconds before or after, any higher or lower, it would have been me. But it wasn't me—it was somebody else."

Still absorbed in his grim recollections of Vietnam, Dan sat down in his chair and lit a cigarette. "You know," he said, "I was in the field eight months before I saw a base camp." He stopped, shook his head slowly, and went on. "To see how quickly a person's life can terminate—as fast as that—and to see one of your buddies get it, it's a hell of a thing. To see a guy die in the rain, so many, many, many, many miles away from any familiar things, any loved ones, just so far away and alone. Life doesn't have any value in cases like that.

"We'd get in a fight and kill some VC's—maybe fifteen or twenty of them. And then we'd go around and take just everything they had. You can get valuable information from the way a guy is dressed, how much food he had, did he have new shoes, what kind of rifle—and when you're through, you just throw—*people*, you know—in a pile, and go off and leave them. And that's the way they treat us too. Sometimes, instead of taking a watch off a dead VC's wrist, a G.I. would just cut off a guy's arm.

"It makes you value and appreciate your being alive. I think I'm a much stronger, an overall easier person, than I used to be. But I'm not as tolerant. I lose my temper; don't have the patience I used to have. I find it harder to focus my attention for any amount of time, harder to read a book. I've started five or ten books and closed the pages and looked at TV or something like that. My thoughts don't come as easily now. Although I feel I'm a better person, I've lost some things, things that came so easy for me once upon a time."

Bridges told me that he hoped to complete his BA degree the next summer and then continue to work in Student Personnel. But he seemed to be less interested in discussing his vocational plans than in explaining how it is a very different experience to be black in Vietnam and black in the United States.

"Here in the States, you as a white man can tell me 'Shut up, nigger' or anything you want, because you have power backing you up. But over in Vietnam, you don't come talking that way to me. Because, in a combat situation, the black man has a pistol too, and he might just be inclined to say, 'Blow it out your nose.' Over there, instead of the white man being one thousand feet on top of you, he's only five hundred feet on top of you. Of course, he still has the essential bargaining power. He still has the ability to compute your actions, but your ability to resist over there is a little bit better.

"I think Vietnam is the best thing that ever happened to a white man. He's been able to associate closer to the black man than here. He's in a position where he can see the black man *for a man*. All privates, black or white, have exactly the same thing: nothing. All sergeants have the same thing: nothing. It's just the man.

"Everybody had some time to do, some days to do, and you started the countdown. Everybody, black or white, has this in common in Vietnam: he has three hundred and sixty-five days to do. We all had this common dream, going home in X number of days. Everybody in the United States should see Vietnam. Not to be exposed in a combat situation, but exposed to Vietnam. Then they would be more grateful for the things they take for granted—a table, a light bulb, everything, anything."

I asked Dan if he had ever had close white friends.

He thought a moment before answering.

"Oh, hell yes. In college there was a Jewish kid. He was a real buddy. The last time I was in New York I stayed with him. He's a great buddy. He was my closest white friend ever. Very few black people are as close to me as he was."

Dan laughed, enjoying his private recollections.

"And there was another white guy in Vietnam—Thomas— he was a good guy. He was a little puny guy and he wanted to do everything everyone else did. He was a great guy to have around. Once I beat him out of his whole check playing poker, but I had to give it back, he was such a—I don't know—was just a great little guy."

Charles Stuyvesant served as a staff sergeant in the Air Force in Vietnam in 1966–67. He was in the psychiatric corps, involved in group psychotherapy sessions, electric shock therapy, insulin shock therapy, and helping to implement behavior toward patients that might prove helpful. He has short blond hair ("this is the longest I have ever worn my hair," he said) and wears sideburns. As we talked, he smoked a pipe or held it in his hand, and was wearing a green sweater, an open-neck shirt, dark slacks. On his hands were two rings, a high school graduation one ("I'll replace it with my college ring") and an amethyst ring he bought in Hawaii while in the service.

Stuyvesant, who is twenty-six, is a senior at a state university in Wisconsin, majoring in psychology, and plans to attend a graduate business school. He also plans to marry his fiancée in a year.

"I think I'll go with big business for a while for the exposure," he told me. "Then come back to a small business where I can be more effective as a decision maker. If I could project myself ahead ten years, I'd say I'll be the president of a business organization with two to five million dollars in net sales. I've always had a life plan. Even when I was a kid, I knew I wanted to study psychology. I've done almost everything I wanted to do. I seem to be able to accomplish what I really set out for."

Charles has a serious manner, and does not smile often; while engaged in conversation, he looks directly into the other person's eyes. When he does smile, it is with openness and warmth.

"I was born and raised on a farm in Wisconsin," he said. "It's an area where such things as self-confidence and individualism are still stressed, and inculcated into a young man growing up. It makes a sharp contrast with the role a military man has to play, and this gave me great frustration, anxiety, and bitterness."

Perhaps because he knew I was a priest, Stuyvesant felt impelled to explain his attitude toward religion. "I don't have a religious background," he said, "at least as far as formal church is concerned. My brothers are Baptist, my sister is Congregationalist. I guess you could say that the Protestant ethic is strong in my family and community, but I don't want to join an organized church, at least, not yet. But I'm a religious man, a very religious man. My convictions revolve around my Maker. To begin with, I'm very grateful for being alive. It's just marvelous. I don't take any day or anything for granted. To me the fact that you can't get away from is that there had to be someone to make all this. That force, however you explain it, is the amazing thing.

"Vietnam perhaps heightened my sense of appreciation for life. I was constantly confronted with examples of just and unjust behavior by men. I was forced to recognize that man is often unjust in his acts. That heightened my appreciation that nations can act like men and be unjust in what they do.

"But I have a great deal of hope. I'm essentially an optimist. In history we see nations rising and falling, but I believe we, as Americans, are going to continue as a nation technologically, and I hope morally. The awareness of men who have been in Vietnam has been sharpened, so that there's going to be a desire to bring about a more moral, a more justified attitude, on the part of our government. This also pertains to the awareness of families of men who died in Vietnam."

I had been told that Stuyvesant was working with various veterans' organizations and asked him whether the young Vietnam veterans and the older veterans of other wars were able to relate to each other.

"Well, there's a conflict between them," he admitted. "The conflict hinges on issues of patriotism—you know, our country, right or wrong. You've got to remember that returning World War II veterans were met as heroes who had done something positive for their country. The Vietnam veteran is much more against this war and has been made more hostile toward any war. People are having their image expectations shattered. For example, at least on this campus, the young antiwar activists include many veterans; that's a dramatic switch from earlier.

"I belong to the American Legion here. They staged a march in town as a counteraction to the war moratorium. Well, I can't support that; I'm for the moratorium. I'm in direct conflict with the older veterans on that. But I'm not going to branch off from the organization. I'll work within the structure and try to change it internally."

Stuyvesant kept emphasizing the importance of the different public attitudes that he and other Vietnam veterans must face, in contrast to those encountered by World War II and Korean War veterans.

"At the university in my classes—I have several group seminars in which we're quite close—the reaction I get when I tell them I'm a Vietnam veteran is, 'What a fool you were to do that.' I get feelings of anger and feelings of alienation; there is a terrible need to explain. But they cut me off and don't want to hear about it. If this only came from the young men, I'd understand it, but the women feel the same way. I represent a disgusting and distasteful situation to them. I seem to personify a professional killer hired by the U. S. Government."

I asked Charles to tell me what his attitude toward the war, and the Vietnamese people, was when he arrived in Vietnam in the fall of 1966.

"I had some extremely strong reactions," he said, "both to the Vietnamese people and the American military. There was shocking poverty in the country. The people were quite naïve in regard to political systems. I got the impression they didn't care whether they had a communist or a socialist or a democratic system, just as long as the war stopped. At the same time, many of those in the cities had a vested economic interest in wanting the war to continue, in order to go on making a profit.

"I made an effort, on one occasion, to try to explain to a Vietnamese college student why we were there. He attended a college in Hue. He was as baffled as many of the Americans were as to the reasons. He was sure we had ulterior motives, rather than just wanting to help the Vietnamese people. He felt the military-industrial complex he's heard about was making a lot of money off the armaments. He also thought it was an imperialist-colonialist policy that brought us there, and that we had a vested interest in building bases to contain Red China."

Charles lit his pipe and began smoking calmly, as he explained his own rationale for Vietnam. "At that particular time," he conceded, "I was baffled as to what our reasons were. I had seen some contradictory things happen. And there were contradictory opinions among U.S. military men about bombing the harbor and railroad lines coming south out of Haiphong. I heard that a colonel and two majors were admitted to the psychiatric ward ostensibly because they had had a very stressful situation. In reality, this wasn't the case at all. They had been on a mission and strafed a Russian cargo ship in the Haiphong harbor. They were put in the psychiatric ward in case an international incident arose for the U.S.—in effect, to give the government an excuse.

"This showed me we had the capability to close the

harbor, yet we never did it. I continued to have ambivalent feelings about both our motives and our tactics. I still do. When you're in uniform, you can't resolve such a question, because you don't have access to the information that would help. Outside the military, back here in the States, you have access to more diversified information systems. Our news is not as controlled here as it was in Vietnam."

What did he feel about the war now?

"I think we went about our strategy in the wrong way. It is *their* war. We can arm them and equip them, but we can't fight it for them. Because it's a civil war.

"We don't need to base our foreign policy on the assumption that we are our brother's keeper. Not that we wouldn't want to, but it doesn't seem to work out in reality."

Beyond all disagreements about the reasons for the war, and the strategy pursued, Stuyvesant was emphatic about the total inadequacy of the preparation he received for what he found in Vietnam.

"Before we were sent over there, we weren't shown films of the countryside, or given opposing views to why we were going there, or even told *why* we were going. The men get the idea they're just in Vietnam to do a job; if they don't do it, they face courtmartial and punishment.

"The motherhood and apple pie—the American dream—turned out to be empty. The reality started to hit home that the war was unjust. Some men deserted and went to Sweden. I thought about that a little, but didn't do it. I probably didn't consider it seriously. I was afraid to speak out against the war for fear of being punished. As far as the men who deserted in Vietnam are concerned, they had justifiable reasons for doing what they did; I don't look down on them at all.

"All I'd been prepared for was to deal with American servicemen who had had an emotional problem brought on by the war. I hadn't been given political briefings or the appropriate background politically. I found it a very shocking situation in that I wasn't prepared to deal with the Vietnamese people—to see their suffering, and the tremendous differences in economic opportunity. I dealt with it by being frustrated—that is, by not dealing with it, for I had a feeling that I didn't seem able to do anything to help."

Stuyvesant seemed to have a great desire to talk, and then would ask whether our interview had any point. "I don't think," he said, "that the American public will ever understand what happened in Vietnam.

"Eventually, lots of people are going to have a good deal of hostility realizing they were duped, when real information begins to leak back, and starts to flow, and then floods. You can tell by certain things now that the complacency of the news media is being shaken. Some people in the media seem to be concerned at last about bringing the realities of the war home. We're getting more accurate reporting of what a war is like. I felt like thanking whoever it was that gave permission a couple of weeks ago to show a TV film recording the killing of a North Vietnamese captive. I hope people who thought of the war as a faraway thing were shocked sufficiently for them to do something to stop it. I'm not sure, however, that the public's understanding of the war will ever reach the proportions it would have if the fighting had continued at 1966–67 levels. So the full reality of Vietnam will be effectively suppressed by the Nixon Administration's phasing out of the war."

Charles was bitter about the whole system of military control, not merely the war in Vietnam. He wanted to know why soldiers had no rights. "Enlisted men," he said, "are no better off than Negroes in Alabama before civil rights. How a young fellow feels about his rights can best be illustrated by this incident. One day we had a man brought into the psychiatric ward who was a young trainee. He had cut his wrists, making what we called a hesitation cut to get out of the very stressful training environment. He was examined by psychiatrists who felt he had a character disorder and was responsible for his acts. He was courtmartialed, the charge being destruction of U.S. Government property. It gave me a lot of insight into what rights I had—when your body belongs to the U.S. Government.

"I think it's a good example of the injustice of the whole setup. It was a comedy of errors, unjust from the first day to the last. I'll always be bitter about being an enlisted man. I'm task-oriented and somewhat capable, and in the army I had to underachieve."

I was worried that we'd left out something crucial and asked Charles if there was some important question I had failed to ask.

"I think the majority of the Vietnam veterans would ask themselves one final thing," he replied. "It is this: 'Would we accept the military environment again if we were called back in another war?' What isn't realized is that there is a widely held attitude of men coming back from Vietnam that, even if for some reason—a foreign government invading our coast, or for any other reason—war was declared by our government and we were asked to serve again, under no circumstances would we be a member of the armed forces of the United States."

There was a long pause. Charles grasped his pipe in his hand tightly. "What will be done by the fellows returning?" he asked himself. "It's too soon to know, but there's a sense that something needs to be done—and a willingness. . . ."

"I was called a Communist this summer in an American Legion club because of my moustache," Hugh Hodges told me. "The guy said 'Are you one of those goddamn commie radicals?' He bragged that he wouldn't let his son have anything but a crew cut."

Hodges, who is twenty-four, is a senior at a college in Michigan. He served in Vietnam in 1966–67. He has a gaunt, lean face that breaks open when he laughs.

"I wonder if it says what I feel?" he asked me.

"It's an Abe Lincoln, frontier face," I replied, admiring his very neat moustache and full head of hair. "Besides, your hair isn't very long."

"Not long?" Hugh repeated. "Ask my parents."

For our interview over coffee in a room inside the college student center, Hugh was wearing a blue shirt and lean checkered slacks. On one of his fingers was a fraternity ring. "It was something I thought I missed when I went to Junior College," he explained. "If you forget about the typical bullshit and go along for the few friends you'll find, it's all right."

Hugh's eyes were haunted, hunted; I asked if he knew he blinked his right eye a great deal. "I wasn't aware of it," he laughed, "but I'm a very tense, very nervous person. Besides, I smoke too much" (two packs a day).

As he speaks, he drums his fingers on a chair. "My dad was in the army for ten years, so I always had an extremely high idea of the service. Before I went in, I was the narrow-minded, sports-crazy kid."

Hodges enlisted in the army in August, 1964, and was sent to Europe as a clerk the next year. He volunteered for Vietnam but heard nothing.

"So I wrote a letter *demanding* that I be sent to Vietnam as my patriotic duty. I got to Vietnam in February, 1966.

"All those big grandiose ideas I had that war is beautiful —medals all over your chest—slipped away when they put me in a Saigon office, where I worked thirteen hours a day. I saw all the bitterness between the Vietnamese people and the Americans, but I still thought—since that is what I had been told—that we were there to fight communism.

"Then I volunteered for the field, the MACV (Military Assistance Command Vietnam). We worked in an advisory capacity with Vietnamese infantrymen. That way I got to see the relationship between an American G.I. and a South Vietnamese G.I. Our job was to help them help themselves. We found out we were doing almost all of the work. It was a real big year of frustration. It was a little like going down to a ghetto with a lot of big ideas, and failing completely.

"We ran the railroad—believe it or not, there *is* a railroad from Saigon to Hue. Nine-tenths of it didn't run. Our job was to defend it, and there were a number of American engineers with new devices. I learned the cardinal rule: we owned the railroad in the day, the Vietcong owned it at night; and, if they really wanted it in the daytime, they could get it then, too. They let it run because it transported their people as well as ours."

Hugh took a cigarette out of his pack on the table and lit it. "The saddest thing I ever saw was the Saigon railroad depot after the Vietcong walked in one night, sent all the people—including the guards—home, and blew up fourteen locomotives. It made me wonder: you're supposed to be helping someone, but if they just walked away like that without any resistance at all, what were we doing there? Were we forcing our way on them?"

With these experiences, what had he thought of the Vietnamese people?

"I hated all Vietnamese," he said flatly. "I thought of them at that time as slant-eyed bastards, lazy, good-for-nothing cheats who were there to use you. The worst thing was once they left a friend of mine, who was wounded, for dead. Things changed, and later I learned to empathize with them, too. It became clear that the United States is there to defend the South Vietnamese government, not the people. You could always tell who was an official in Saigon—he was the one who had the new car or the mansion. It used to make me sick to see a South Vietnamese officer walk in, not caring for his men, and trying to get some high-class champagne for a party he was throwing.

"The Vietnamese couldn't care less about democracy or communism or anything else. They just want to be left alone. They don't know what's going on except that if the Vietcong move in some area, then the Americans will go after them, and the guy who loses the most will be the farmer, the ordinary peasant.

"When you're over there as a G.I., you start to get paternalistic, in spite of yourself. You know, 'I'm going to *help* them and they'd damned better be grateful.' You don't *see* that you're walking across some guy's bean patch, and that that's his whole life. You just know he doesn't want you and it makes you damned mad."

Hodges poured himself another cup of coffee, before telling me an illustrative anecdote.

"One day, when we were out on reconnaissance, I had a carbine over my shoulder. Suddenly I felt a tug—this South Vietnamese was trying to steal my ammunition! I smiled at him and told him 'No.' He smiled back and offered to buy it from me. I said 'No' again, naturally, but later I asked a captain with me why the guy wanted it. The captain said he'd either sell it on the black market or else use it himself, because the South Vietnamese rationed ammo.

"We were hated by every Oriental. The only interest they had in us was for our dollars. In a way, we were fighting an unseen enemy. You take someone like I was at the time— young, naïve—and what is the army going to say to him? It can't say, 'You're wasting your time.' So it says, 'You're here to fight for the American flag.' It almost makes you forget you are ten thousand miles away from the American flag."

How had Hugh's ideas changed since he had returned from Vietnam and come to the campus?

"When I came back, I was playing the role of a gung-ho veteran hard-ass. Someone would tell me about a friend dying in Vietnam, and I was almost callous enough to say 'That's the way it goes.'

"The first year back it was still all black and white, but lots of controversy churning around inside me. I would argue the domino theory—you know, if we don't stop them there, they'll be in California tomorrow. I remember a kid talking about the horrors of the war, and I'd be polishing him off with my arguments. Of course, it's easier to argue the domino theory than the morality of the war. Actually, I was almost a right-winger for about a year when I got back. I thought the poor were poor because they were lazy, and I was anti-black."

Hugh's development became a great deal more understandable after he told me about his early background.

"I came from a small, pretty well all-white town in western Ohio. My parents had no conscious feeling one way or the other about race—let's just say they never talk about it. My racial attitude hardened while I was serving in Germany. Black GI's would get together in groups and it seemed to me they were always loud and boisterous. This turned me off. Apparently it was all right for a bunch of white guys to get drunk, but not black guys. Maybe this is a part of the ingrown white American experience.

"I could never empathize with blacks before I got back from Vietnam and met a college teacher, my own age—we'd have a few beers after class and just talk—and he gave me books to read, some of Bernard Fall, and Harrington's *The Other America*. A great change took place in me. It stemmed from a focal point of religious change.

"I'd been a Roman Catholic all my life. My father was Lutheran and my mother Roman Catholic; today she's a Lutheran, too. I attended church dutifully in Vietnam; now I understand why. I believed the Roman Catholic Church was the only church, the true church, and this was the only way to heaven. When I had doubts, I would shut them off.

"Two books did a great deal for me—Tillich's *Dynamics of Faith* and Joseph Fletcher's *Situation Ethics*. I began to realize the fallacy of my old religion, that I had been a Catholic out of fear. I had believed that if I went against any teachings of my church I would go to hell.

"I've never felt better in my life than now. I try to examine every situation as to whether it's right or wrong. It's so much easier to live with the idea of *agape* than structural law. Nothing turns me off more than going to a church service and sitting next to someone who is muttering and doesn't know what he's saying."

After he had been back from Vietnam for about a year, Hodges's attitudes about the war changed considerably, and a bumper sticker on his car read: "How Many Vietnamese Fought in Our Civil War?" He told me of an encounter with a college alumnus, an older man, who took note of the bumper sticker, as well as Hugh's long hair, and indignantly asked a school administrator who "the goddamn radical bastard" was. "You mean Hugh?" the administrator supposedly replied, with a deadpan expression on his face. "You've got to go easy on him; he only got back from fighting in Vietnam fourteen months ago." The alumnus walked away, Hugh reported, without saying another word.

I tried to get Hodges to concretize his position on the war: what were our options? Should America simply get out of Vietnam?

"It's no simple issue," he replied. "You can't say America is wrong in being there because you don't really know enough: you're just one person.

"I worked for Eugene McCarthy's campaign in sixty-eight, but I was glad he didn't get nominated because of what he said afterward. He wanted to get all the American troops out of Vietnam in six months, and that's economically and militarily impossible. Everybody asks me, 'How do you get out of Vietnam?' and I have to answer, 'How do I know?'

"I wish the New Left types on campus would recognize the difference between the army and the man in it: a giant machine and the G.I. struggling to survive. While I'm against the war in every way, I can empathize with the guys fighting over there. I wish there was some way you could make liberal, upper-middle-class kids, who are against the war (who think 'Pig' when they see a cop *or* a G.I.) could realize they don't understand what the hell the G.I. has gone through in Vietnam."

Hugh's estimate of the peace movement as a whole was also double-edged. "Most of the people in it are peace-loving, I guess, and when they say, 'We have to get out,' or 'The Establishment is wrong,' that's okay; but too often they almost seem to be laughing at the G.I. sitting in the middle of the jungle being shot. How do you laugh at the guy caught in that situation? And how can you claim to be peace-loving if you feel hatred for the ordinary soldier? If a person believes, really believes it when he says, 'I'm making the world safe for democracy,' shouldn't you have something better to say to him than 'You're full of shit'?

"There's a need to get both sides up on the speaker's platform. People have got to learn to listen rationally, pulling something out of each argument. I've run the gamut from right to left on the war; now I'm sort of a liberal moderate. The war in Vietnam is too complicated to hear only one side.

"Like a girl last night said to me, 'How do you expect me to say Vietnam is wrong when my brother is over there right now?' And how do you tell a mother, 'Your son was killed over there and it was all a mistake—he died in vain'? When you're dealing in human emotions, you've got to do *more*. I've found out there's no such thing as absolute right or wrong anymore, some things are more right or more wrong, but black and white answers don't make sense."

Hodges majors in American Studies, plans to attend graduate school, and wants to teach in college. He has no plans now for marriage: "I couldn't afford a wife. I'm even going to have to borrow from my parents next semester to pay my school bills and I hate like hell to do it." In the meantime, he has a part-time job as a probation officer for the local municipal court. "I'm working with mostly black kids around my age who are in trouble and need someone to talk to. Fortunately, the judge is a remarkable person who realizes it's no answer to throw somebody in jail. The kids can't talk to the usual probation officer, but I'm at least the same age as they are, use the same jargon they do, wear jeans and sandals, have long hair and a moustache."

Understandably, Hugh was discouraged by the absence of visible results. "Frankly, I find the whole thing depressing as hell. It's another Vietnam, walking in with all these grandoise ideas of saving, and failing. Nothing gets accomplished when you've got hostile black people and prejudiced white police-men; it's hopeless. Each side is equally wrong.

"And then, last summer, I worked in a construction crew painting bridges. There was a white kid in the group, about twenty years old, and he chews me out, 'Hugh, your genera-tion failed.' *My* generation! I asked him what he was talking about and he said, 'You clowns screwed it all up. You're a racist. You still believe in integration.' Boy, I blew up. God, all of a sudden you find we're going back to the old separate but equal idea."

I had been struck by what Hugh had said of a significant religious change that had taken place recently in him, and asked for more details.

"I worked out something for myself over the last year and a half. My religion (I hate to use clichés, but I guess you have to) is something like the brotherhood of man. I try to practice it. It's so much better to look for the good points in a person or a situation. It's kind of fun not to talk behind some-one else's back. Someone else has his own problems and is better than you are in many ways. It brings back what a base-ball player told me once, that he never met a man he couldn't learn from.

"My roommate now is a very staunch Christian and we have arguments all the time. I feel God cannot be categorized, the old pie in the sky idea is gone. Everyone has his own central theme, his idea of why he exists, and I think this is what God is for him. What turned me away from organized religion is this idea of a God who puts man on earth and gives him a free will and then restrains him with fear of punishment. I don't believe in hell anymore, but I think I believe in an afterlife. What it is, I don't know, but it's *not* torture."

Because of what other veterans had said, I asked Hugh how had he been received on the college campus?

"In the beginning," he said, "people didn't say 'There's Hugh' but 'There's a Vietnam veteran.' But now they say 'There's Hugh.' I used to eat it up—the idea that I was a patriotic celebrity, but then I got embarrassed because the war is just a part of me.

"I wore blinders when I walked into the army. They fell off when I walked out. Now, because of my courses and discussions with friends at college, I'm able to utilize what I lived through in a more intellectual way.

"Someone said to me, 'You don't act like a veteran. You act like one of the guys.' I said, 'I *am* one of the guys. I'm a college senior like you are.' Some of the kids didn't like me because I'd go out and drink and be a college student. I wasn't supposed to be a college student but a symbol. It's kind of nice now not having to live up to all that."

After our interview, I joined Hugh and some other students for a spaghetti lunch in an Italian restaurant near the campus. Hugh and I sat beside one another in a booth, directly across from two younger men who wore extremely long hair and held semiradical views about the war and America's long-range priorities. Lifestyles clashed in visible conflict while the restaurant jukebox nearly drowned out most conversation.

I cut through the noise to ask Hugh how long he expected the war in Vietnam to last.

"As long as there's democracy and communism, there's going to be a physical conflict. I can't envision us getting out of Vietnam within twenty-five years—maybe not for fifty years. I *see* us in Vietnam. That's the focal point of this half of the century. It's a tragedy, the Vietnam people are almost totally forgotten. Vietnam is a symbol. Maybe America will have a second focal point—even three or four focal points—but I think Vietnam is here to stay."

Would he go back to Vietnam as a fighting man?

Hugh shifted in his chair and lit another cigarette.

"I have one more year to go in a six-year commitment. So I'm now classified Reserve Available, which is 1 R. But if they called me back for duty in Vietnam, I would refuse to go. I'm not exactly sure why I wouldn't go. I went the first time because I believed in it, thought it was necessary. But fundamentally I don't believe in what is going on there now and I refuse to go along with it. To thine own self be true. If I went back, I wouldn't be true and I'd end up frustrated again."

Suddenly, there was a moment's quiet between records and Hodges's voice was louder than he intended.

"Everybody asks, 'What is Vietnam like?'" he said. "It's like saying 'What is life like?' They don't want to know what my mind is like. Yet the important thing, really, is what my mind is thinking about Vietnam."

John Vislocki is twenty-three years old, married, and a graduate student in Art at a college in Indiana. He was drafted in October, 1967, a few months after completing his undergraduate work. John has a full head of brown hair, wears sideburns with a neat moustache, and was dressed in an open-neck sports shirt, plain slacks, and loafer shoes. Looking at me through black horn-rimmed glasses, he always spoke in a restrained voice, alert, understated, and quietly intense.

"If you mention you're a veteran of Vietnam, people say, 'Well, you made it back,' and that's all," he began. "Nobody wants to talk about it or really hear about it."

I asked him why he thought this was so.

"It's a number of things. If it's a student, he doesn't want to think about the possibility of going there someday. Many Americans are ashamed of what's going on there, but the fact is that not too many people know how much of a shame it really is.

"I was appalled at the American lives wasted there, young men down the drain, to no visible purpose. And all the money. Most people seem to try to erase it from their minds unless they're involved in it, you know, unless they've had a son or relative over there."

John's sense of needless waste was obvious, but did he feel that he understood the issues involved in Vietnam?

"I came back last July," he said. "I don't have any idea what it's all about—that is, in terms of what our aims are. It's so confusing. You hear somebody say, 'To try to stop the red tide.' And some of the young G.I.'s have the old patriotic idea, that the reds will be in San Diego tomorrow if they're not stopped right away.

"But the older G.I.'s are very critical. They've seen so many blunders being made. And they know that, on the part of the South Vietnamese, there's not much appreciation"—he smiled to emphasize his point—"of course, they appreciate our money. They've been fighting for so long over there that it's just a part of their lives. And the Cong, they're even more set in their purpose than the South Vietnamese. They grab young men at fourteen and fifteen and make them serve. But you can't make men engage in suicide attacks on bases unless they believe what they're doing.

"I've seen these raids. The enemy will attempt to break in at night and destroy whatever they can. One night they broke into our camp and got six trucks and one howitzer. They hurt us a lot. When you see these young men with bombs taped to their bodies, you know they really believe in their cause and aren't going to quit.

"The South Vietnamese people want us and our money, but they also help the enemy. You're supposedly helping these people, but you know they don't appreciate it, so it makes it hard to put your heart into it."

But what did the American fighting men in Vietnam think about the war?

"The men know the people at home don't have any idea of what's happening. We lose quite badly sometimes and the public doesn't know. You'll hear on the news, 'There was heavy fighting' somewhere—and they'll give the kill number, but no details. The G.I.'s don't want the people at home to worry—because then they get all upset and write you bad letters, and the only thing that keeps you going over there is letters.

"Of course, it's always only for one year—the time served in Vietnam—not the duration. Everybody thinks of how much longer it will be until he can go home. Many G.I.'s will refuse to go out of the bunker at the very end of their year, when there's just a short time left; they refuse to risk their lives any longer."

He lit a cigarette and sat back in his chair. "I'm really quite bitter about the whole thing. I'm not proud of what I had to do over there. To come back and have people not want to say a word about it—to forget this year of your life—is hard.

"I saw young men who didn't want to be there and didn't want to be doing what they were doing, and now they're dead. And their sacrifice isn't appreciated. A veteran is made to feel ashamed of what he has done.

"Invariably, when you make friends over there and they come home, they never write back. I haven't either. What could I say? I left some real friends over there, and I gave them my address and told them to come and visit me. But things are beginning to settle down for me and to write now would only remind them they still have ninety days more. The thing in your mind is what day you're coming home. I wouldn't want to get a letter back from them saying the camp was hit last night and we lost so many men. I'd be troubled about not being there, which wouldn't help them, or me either."

I was curious as to what Vislocki's attitude would be regarding those Americans at home who had demonstrated publicly for peace?

"I want to believe that all the peace people sincerely want to see peace. But hell, some of them would end up as the biggest hawks if they ever got to Vietnam. It's amazing how many Americans have learned to really hate the Vietnamese—Northern, Southern, all of them. I'm not sure what the demonstrations mean. If they're students, maybe it's primarily to change the situation so they won't have to go. On the other hand, G.I.'s tend to say, 'Demonstrators are hippies—send them to the front lines.' But I don't think they really mean it. In a way, they'd like to be demonstrating too."

In contrast to the considerable hostility of the G.I.'s toward the Vietnamese people, John's sympathies were quite friendly. "You go to the villages—the children are great. They've had such a terrible life. You can see the disease and birth defects. You go crazy wondering why the money spent on the war couldn't be spent to help these people live better."

Vislocki was very pessimistic about the influence of the fighting in Vietnam on a postwar America. "I think there will be more violence," he asserted. "Thousands of bitter men have learned to hate people. Keep in mind that most of the fighting is in close, and it's quite bloody. The men get quite hardened, even the young. I've seen a boy of eighteen bayonet a wounded prisoner to death because he didn't want to waste time carrying him. When all these guys get home, I think some of this cold rage will emerge again; in fact, I'm quite sure of it. They go through a village and want to destroy everything in it, and they just go ahead and do it. You can't go through a year of this and come home and return to normal. It's just not possible."

As for the integration of black and white soldiers in Vietnam, Vislocki confirmed what I already knew. "For the main part, they work together. But in leisure time, they congregate separately. And there's still discrimination, even in action. I was in the artillery in an ammunition section where all but one or two of the men were black. It was a bad job and nobody else wanted it, so they got it. They were quite angry, but there wasn't much they could do about it. Unless there was a black sergeant. I ran into more and more black sergeants toward the end of my time there."

Before he entered the service, John's main interest was art. "Even when I was a kid, I was always painting or creating something. For me, the service was a period when I couldn't create. I had to do what I had to do because somebody else said so. I had to stop creating and just try to get along. Now it's hard to get in the groove again; I've lost contact with the art world. My hope is to teach a studio course in a college, whether painting or sculpture or photography.

"I imagine my father and mother were quite upset by my

whole experience in Vietnam. My mother was ill and in the hospital. But they never wrote me about that. I didn't want them to know what was happening. It was a kind of unreal situation.

"I got married while I was in basic training. I'd been going with the girl for five years and didn't want to put it off any longer. I'd applied for OCS and was sent to Ft. Sill, Oklahoma, to the artillery. I started the OCS program but couldn't see spending six months there and adding to my time in the army."

The war had affected Vislocki's approach to religion, too.

"As a kid, I was baptized a Catholic. I remember in my childhood going to catechism but I never received much religious training. When I was in college, and still living at home, my mother and two sisters and I went to a Lutheran church every week, while my father stayed home.

"When I was getting married, since my wife was Catholic, I thought it would be simpler if I was confirmed there. But I don't see how it makes any difference what church you belong to, if you worship God.

"War and religion don't mix too well, I found. Imagine finding yourself on a mountain somewhere in Vietnam; you don't know for how long you'll be there. Occasionally, they'll send out a chaplain and they'll let everybody go to a service. But you begin to realize that you can't worship like you used to, and many G.I.'s didn't want to go even though it meant getting away from the outfit for a while. The chaplain was an officer and a part of the army, so they said 'the hell with it.' "

Vislocki's army training was in the artillery, working with a fire-direction center. "It's five men who work a twelve-hour shift," he explained. "I ran a portable computer. You push the buttons and it gives you the data so that guns can hit their target. We'd fire a couple of thousand rounds of ammunition into an area before the infantry would go in. Sometimes we'd shell an area all day. One area—just a few hundred meters—we just shelled it constantly for three days.

"You'd get a call over the radio. The people out there—you could hear the voices—would need help desperately. But before we could fire a single artillery shot out there, you'd have to get American *and* South Vietnamese clearance. Many times we'd find out our men were shooting at the South Vietnamese or the South Vietnamese were shooting at our men. It was quite a bungle, with so many elements there not working well together."

John stood up, walked over to a window, and looked outside for a moment before resuming his narration.

"I remember one night—a forward observer was getting some artillery shells fairly close to his position. We went through higher channels to find out who was firing. *Nobody*, they told us. But a man was there with his men and the shells were getting closer. Then we found that our higher-ups had cleared that area for the Koreans to fire on but had forgotten about it.

"We'd get a report that fire power was needed. We supplied it and then a call would come back telling us 'You killed an American.' It turned out to be a simple mistake made by someone computing the data. Or a forward observer would be responsible for the error, misled by poor maps and the fact that the terrain was unknown to him. The maps were updated from ones the French had. When you're in the midst of rice paddies or the jungle, it's hard to get your bearings.

"I remember once when we got the data and asked higher command for clearance to fire—someone out there urgently needed help. But we couldn't give him help because an insect sprayer was flying around killing insects. We only had so many radios and you couldn't get clearance."

Vislocki went on to relate other ironies of American technological warfare. "The young guys are listening to rock music on transistors while they're marching. They listen to rock all the time. And many G.I.'s have small portable TV's, and they sit there, glued to the TV, not aware of what was going on around them.

"We went over as a battalion—there were four batteries. There was real competition over the body count, how many Vietnamese had been killed. Many G.I.'s would get excited if word came of enemy who had been spotted crossing a field, because this could greatly increase the body count. But what kind of attitudes are we forming if our guys find it natural to go wipe out a Cong patrol and then go back to listening to the radio? It was such a weird situation I just couldn't believe it.

"Many of the men do turn to pot and dope over there. You can get a package of ten marijuana cigarettes for one dollar, ten cents apiece. Since you need the men to help fight, you can't send them to jail. We had two South Vietnamese who worked with us as interpreters, working with us all the time. One of them was tossed into jail for supplying the whole battery with marijuana. He had a wife and kids, and was supposed to be on our side, but he wasn't really helping. You see, a man has to be only a little bit off when he is working on this kind of data for directing artillery fire, and well, *there* goes a village, or *there* go so many Americans who are killed. With that power, when a man makes a small mistake in his calculations, he can do an awful lot more damage then men could ever do in a war before."

Vislocki didn't think his fellow American fighting men in Vietnam were very politically minded. "There were quite a few discussions on whether we should be there or not. But people were set in their views and nobody could hear anybody else. Besides, your means of getting information over there is—you know, *Stars and Stripes*, the military publication. And you have the Armed Forces Vietnam Radio station with a sergeant for a disc jockey. It's all put there by the army. So it's hard, even while you're over there, to find out what's going on in Vietnam. Besides, what really concerns you is not long-range political factors but an intelligence report about your immediate area—about whether you'll live or die.

"I was working a twelve-hour shift. If we were doing a lot of firing, what with there always being sandbags to fill, and always having to repair things because they rot, I'd get about five hours sleep a day. I was with a group that was more highly educated than the average G.I.; most of them had been to college. But they weren't really concerned about political questions; it was just the big question, how many days were left before you went home?"

The Vietnam experience had made John question war itself. "War really isn't possible now, in this time and age. All the kinds of weapons we have. And all the communications. You'll get a call for help, and it will be cut off by another station. There's too much communication; it leads to hopeless complexity. You can send white phosphorus into a Vietnamese village and it's not there anymore. You make a mistake with that and *people* are burned too. It might definitely get out of hand someday.

"It's quite possible people could destroy themselves. I've seen how strong the feelings of hate and revenge can be. If they have a weapon over there, they're going to use it. We have a policy in Vietnam called *Chieu Hoi*—what we describe as our open-arms policy. The idea is that if a Vietnamese gives himself up to us, we'll find a place for him to work; in effect he's forgiven, and he'll be paid for information. I remember a Vietnamese, who had killed a G.I., gave himself to us under *Chieu Hoi*. The infantry grabbed him and tied a charge to him and blew him up. The G.I.'s had seen what happens to their friends, and it tears them up—out of control. But the revenge is often much worse."

I thanked John for helping me see the psychological complexity of the veterans' perceptions; he only nodded silently, as if he were working out a problem for himself. "You know," he said finally, "in a way I should be grateful; Vietnam made me face reality. Previously I wasn't concerned about what's happening in the world. I was wrapped up in my own thing. It's made me more aware of people—how they love, how they hate, how they kill each other, things like that. I have a larger world now.

"I've seen people try to reason with somebody, asking

him not to fire shells on a village or to shoot. But it's hard to get anyone to listen to you. For they're involved in *their* own thing. So it's hard to know what the answer is.

"I used to have a very violent temper and get excited. I'm a very nonviolent person now. Vietnam has made me value human life and feelings much more than before. But I've seen others go through the same things, and it's made them more violent; they lose concern about others' feelings or lives. Once I heard an officer say, 'Well, let's shoot it anyway because it's body count.' He was referring to a line of Vietnamese peasants, seen from a distance. And if a mistake has been made—if it's a South Vietnamese who has been shot instead of a North Vietnamese—you destroy the identification, using it for enemy body count. So many dead bodies this week. We beat the other guy."

He tried to concentrate on the practical implications of his everyday occupation in combat. "Most of the time, we were inside a bunker, hearing radio calls and firing out into the countryside. It was totally weird to know you'd killed somebody nine miles away by pushing a button. But there I was, pushing buttons. I hate the idea of using mathematics to kill people, instead of a gun. Every few hours a weather report would come down, and we'd use *it* to kill people, too. It was a bad year for me. There's a computer and slide rules and it's just like a very quick math problem—you work out the data very fast, only this time it's to blow away a village. There was no way out.

"I've more or less tried to put the whole thing out of my mind. That's largely why I did so much reading over there—without that, I don't think I could have made it through the year without some drastic changes in myself."

Vislocki stood up to leave, and put out his hand with great dignity.

"I'm really grateful you wanted to talk about this," he said. "You generally look for someone else who's been through the same thing—you want to find someone who already *knows*.

You think you have to seek out another veteran who has been in Vietnam. After they found out where I just came from, it always seemed that other people don't want to talk about it."

I thanked him, and we moved toward the door. "Even my wife," John said, half to himself, "even though she's a registered nurse, I can't bring myself to talk with her. About the suffering and the pain. I don't think I'll ever be able to."

Roy Jones, twenty-three, is presently an undergraduate at a Big-Ten university. He was inducted into the army in September, 1967, and, following advanced infantry training, was sent to Vietnam in February, 1968. He returned to the U.S. a year later. Roy is quite intense, gesturing and laughing as he speaks. Very lean, he has gentle but sharply alert eyes. He talks spasmodically, uttering great clusters of words without taking a breath. He was wearing tight corduroy pants and a sport shirt, and had unruly long hair and a rakish moustache. A brass bracelet hung on his elbow and I asked him if it had come from Vietnam.

"Yes," he said, "from a tribal mountain people in the Nam called the Montagnards. They hate the lowland people and just wander, hiding out and living as best they can. Once they saw some of us and sent a couple of extremely brave representatives down to find out if we meant them harm. They discovered we wouldn't kill them and would give them food. There were about a hundred of them in this particular group.

"They were an intriguing people. I thought they were really neat. You can imagine the differences culturally between us and people who haven't seen an electric light. It was one of them who gave me the bracelet. My arm feels badly if I don't wear it," Roy laughed. "Actually, you know, I'll be safe if any Montagnards come around."

Jones is now organizing a movement of veterans who are concerned about peace. I asked him to explain the process of development that had led to such involvement. "Well," he began slowly, "I opposed the war very strongly even before

I went into the army. Before, I was a pacifist, which I no longer am. I have to admit, in a utilitarian sense, that total pacifism is not viable. There are certain violent acts that might be of benefit to mankind. Logically, I cannot be a pacifist.

"I went right from infantry training in Alabama to the Nam. I was assigned to an infantry company and started to work informally, and sometimes illegally—according to official definitions—on the ameliorative kinds of things you can do even in Vietnam—treating the symptoms rather than the cause. There's a lot of violence that can be prevented in combat, a great deal of it.

"My job in the company was to carry the radio. I'd only been there a little while when we were super-decimated in a mortar ambush. The company was made inoperative because so few people were left. When the company was pulled back, I became the communications chief. This put me in a command post.

"I was carrying a battalion radio, giving me an opportunity to do a lot of things. I tried to suppress conflict to the extent that can be done, which is pretty considerable. I was there for six months."

Jones leaned forward in his chair, as he often did while he talked to me, hunched over and using his hands to express his feelings. I could easily visualize him in hundreds of bull sessions in Vietnam, spinning out his thoughts in long sentences with humor and vivid imagery.

"Then I got a job in the rear at the division training center. As men come into Vietnam, they're sent to a centralized place for initial processing. They get a combat leadership course. The army has been having a lot of trouble in regard to personal, as against divisional leadership. I rather suspect that the higher the stress level, the more guys have turned to personal leadership in the field. My division had finally recognized this, and picked out the real leaders. Since the men would follow them anyhow, they were the ones to get leadership training.

"I taught a variety of things, and this gave me the opportunity to deal with large numbers of men at a time. They let me have pretty total autonomy in what I said. So—I basically pushed the peace approach. I honestly don't understand why they let me go on. I used to teach a lot of techniques for avoiding contact with the enemy, ways and means for avoiding fire fights and things.

"It also gave me an opportunity to push other subjects; they have training in civil affairs—you know, your relations to the people in the Nam. They took a very hard line approach. I'm sure there are a lot of G.I.'s who arrive there, by virtue of the draft, who have no strong opinions about the war in general and the Vietnamese people in particular. Training will build up basic attitudes, in one direction or the other, about these things. I spent a lot of time in rap sessions with the other instructors as well as the troops coming through. Of course, in the broader sense, these were all legal actions on my part."

The idea of Jones training combat leaders how to avoid contact with the enemy sounded like something out of a Vietnamese *Catch-22*, and there was a pause as we both drank some coffee.

"There were a lot of other actions, sometimes a little more dangerous," Jones resumed. "As I got to understand the possibilities, things just grew. For example, the shammers—that's a G.I. word for guys who have been away from their outfits for some legitimate reason but who, through various ways, have been able to extend the time. The military's own estimate was that, for example, over Christmas in sixty-eight, there were four thousand shammers out of fifteen thousand men in a single division. There are always a lot of bullshit reasons given out, but considering the total chaos in the Nam, there's no way to check if the guy cheated or not. You can't run it down.

"There are various kinds of shammers. One is a wound shammer. He's well enough to come back but, for various reasons, does not. It involves any excuse for getting out of the field and into the rear for goofing off. The percentage of people getting wounded in the Nam is extremely high. The number of people killed doesn't really indicate the level of fighting. Nearly everyone I know has been wounded once or twice. If, every time a man was wounded, they had to get a new draftee from the States, the situation would be very uncool.

"So we have all these shammers running wild all over the Nam. This is why the attitude given to new troops is so important. In companies, the percentage of absenteeism varies. A strong antiwar attitude helps them to follow their natural tendency to avoid the field. The platoon was nonfunctional most of the time. It was so bad, the platoon leaders were shammers too, so the leader would change every two or three weeks.

"With all these shammers running around, they've got to have food, a place to stay, and the right paper work to protect them. Through various means—it's amazing what can be done, there's so much confusion, people by the thousands are coming in and going out every day—we sheltered and fed and otherwise provided for these shammers in the rear areas. Basically, the problem is to hide them, which is not to make them remote but to blend them easily into groups of people."

Jones explained how a basic psychological factor of army life could be used by antiwar G.I.'s to convert new men to their point of view. "All through army life, one of the most important influences is the guy who's been there longer than you have. The army has an extremely good gut understanding of psychiatry. It not only has the cumulative experience of thousands of years of military life, but it's done some extremely good studies of psychiatry—a lot of this is classified and hasn't been released.

"One thing the army does is not let a man know what's going to happen the next day. They try to make sure you learn from no one but them. However, one of the results of this is that almost everybody is frantic to know what's going to happen. The guy who's been there two days is a real authority to the guy who's been there one day. The guy who's been there five weeks is an authority to the guy who's been there three weeks. You can imagine the extent to which this goes on in the Nam.

"You've got this eighteen-year-old. He is asking questions. Being a new guy is a very uncomfortable thing; it's probably the most uncomfortable thing I've ever experienced. People who have already been there become a tremendous reference source to you. They teach you every aspect of your life. The first two weeks you learn literally thousands of things they didn't teach you in basic training. You are taught your opinions as well as the facts.

"The ten men you live with in your squad are the strongest possible unit. I had friendships there so close I never knew anything like it before or after. To say that an antiwar squad converts a new man is an understatement. It means to give him a whole new set of attitudes, not merely opinions—they change his whole lifestyle."

I asked Jones what he believed an organization of veterans concerned about peace might be able to accomplish in America.

"People as a whole are not perceptive," he began. "The government has done a remarkable job of distorting and covering up the reality of the Vietnam experience. The mere fact that the government has said it is still considered truth by millions. Despite the fact men have been coming back from the Nam saying highly critical things from the beginning, it isn't getting through.

"I think organizing G.I.'s and veterans is most important. For people who currently believe in the war, and are taken in by the weird myth of the uniform and 'our boys' overseas, it's crucial to *use* that image. Okay patriots, your boys in uniform and overseas believe the war is a lot of garbage. They are, as a matter of fact, your next-door neighbors, the ones with the biggest flag poles. They went over to Vietnam and they think the war is a lot of shit.

"A G.I. or veterans' organization has to end some dangerous myths. The military is able to make everything secret—'*We* know this is necessary'—and people swallow that. Part of our responsibility as ex-G.I.'s is to show the public how the military deliberately lies to the public.

"If you deal just with ending the war, you're dealing with symptoms and not the cause. Some people say, 'It was just a good, honest mistake—we should pull out so that no one else is killed—' But it was not a good, honest mistake! It was a manifestation of a whole complex of attitudes and ideas which are propagated by some very powerful interests. We need to be made aware of the structure of these things, and that the Nam is only a brother of a lot of other things going on, including our general repressive outlook, weird international policy, poverty, and racism. It's malevolent even when it isn't erupting into another war. So I'm interested in things G.I.'s can do. Our priorities have got to be reordered."

Was he hopeful that significant changes could be made?

"I'm not hopeful in the way a lot of people are. Judging by the intense energy level being exerted and the sacrifices people are ready to make, however, I expect things to happen. Radicals as a whole are getting a lot more sophisticated in their tactics. We're finally learning that the way to approach things is not to play the part of the martyr. The system has an inexhaustible capacity to punish. There are other ways to work for change, ways even the system has to pay attention to.

"One reason I'm hopeful is that most of the college radicals I know are aware of the fact that the campus isn't very important anymore. We've got to spread into the factory and the army and other places that used to seem unpromising.

"Does a man lose his civil rights just because he's drafted into the army? You're not giving men the rights they're supposed to be fighting for—freedom of speech and assembly and press. The army has taken some very stupid repressive measures. They have to make an army prison worse than just being in the army; people are even refused basic things like food and water; the beatings are incredible. I've known quite a few people who have been in army prisons in the Nam, and some who have come out have been made psychotic. In the Nam they have to make being in prison in the Nam worse than being in the Nam. But you'll be seeing a lot of change coming in the army."

Hoping to account for Roy's ideas, I asked for more information about his family background, and educational and religious formation.

"I'm originally from Iowa," he said. "My mother is a high-school teacher; my father works for a trucking company. They're both moderates politically. They both believe in God, but they're not fanatics about it, and they don't go to church.

"When I was in third or fourth grade, I decided the God story was pretty unlikely. For a while I thought I might be the only person in the world who didn't believe in God. I haven't ever got back to God, but I don't feel God's been a very good force in the world. In the past couple of years, however, there's been a resurgence among some religious people who have suddenly burst out into the streets where the people are. I've been pretty impressed by this.

"I dropped out of school three years ago—I was studying to be a psychologist—because I knew you learn more out of school than in—yes, even academically! I was losing my education by being in school, reading the things assigned to me.

"Actually, I started college when I was seventeen as a philosophy major. I became a utilitarian, and this compelled me to accept the logical consequences of that; so, as a utilitarian, I could no longer be a philosopher. I was so naïve that I went in as a philosophy major to find a philosophy. I found it and I left."

When I asked Roy what he wanted to do with his life, he laughed.

"That's a good question. A few years ago, I was dropping out, little by little. Then I drifted around; I thought it would clear my head. Then I got older and became aware of a lot of things. When I got out of the army, I just walked around for six months. In the Nam you spend maybe twenty dollars a month and the rest you save. So I had money to take care of myself. I got involved in a lot of radical causes. Now that I'm back in school, most of my courses seem generally naïve, and I'm learning a lot of things that are not true in many ways. I came back to school because I thought I wanted to do the academic thing, but now I don't. However, in school I can relate to a fair number of quite interesting people.

"I consider the time I spent in the Nam the most important part of my whole life. My whole being is different from when I went into the army. The people I knew before, I can't even talk to them anymore, because I'm not the same. I had had a very serious relationship with a girl—it had gone on for four years—now that's all over."

How would Roy sum up what happened to him in Vietnam?

"What happened to me?" He hunched forward in the chair and thought about it. "You can't say it. You can't express it in any way. I know some people back from the Nam who are really strange, who are weird. The experience has changed the whole structure of their minds.

"I find it harder to sympathize with the people in this country now because they're so unrealistic. The Vietnamese are so different. The first six months after getting out of the army, I even tried to go back there. But I realized that was escapist. People here are so rich and so far removed from the realities of the world. They have so many things to shield themselves from other people's feelings. They're so jaded.

"Can you imagine how different an environment it is when night comes and it's dark and quiet, and all night long is dark and quiet, all you hear is leaves rustling, a hissing sound from the radio, and once an hour the guard changes? You take enjoyment out of different things when you live at a tremendously reduced living standard. You sleep on the ground. If it rains you get wet. C rations—you may eat the same meal every meal for quite a while. You learn what it's like to carry a twenty-pound radio and thirty pounds of other kinds of shit on your back. Most people here don't even know what sweat tastes like.

"When you remove old stimuli, your mind goes in different places. It's a tremendously productive experience, at least it was for me. You look inside. It completely changes you. You're so much more sensitive. Your senses are at such a level that very small stimuli become very big things.

"I remember, after we'd been in the field for two months, we came into a little landing zone. A place out in the wilderness gouged into a hill. At night the G.I.'s inside bunkers had candles, which couldn't be seen from outside. But standing right there on the ground, suddenly we saw twenty bunkers with candles lit, and our minds just freaked out. It was beautiful—an event. You don't look at TV and movies there. Nobody comes to stimulate you; you stimulate each other. You learn to relate to other people.

"Then you come back to the States and people think you're like them and you're not. You talk about the same things they do, but you see them so differently. Now my senses are getting calloused again. If I'd been in the Nam and seen just one blinking neon light—I mean, wow—and now I see streets of them, and they don't impress me.

"Death and blood are unreal at first, and then they're very real. This means a very different perception about your outlook on life. It means you're going to die. I didn't use to know it. Not sensing you're going to die, you don't realize you're alive. Maybe that's the thing I learned in the Nam: I learned I'm alive."

I knew he was saying something important, something that neither he nor I had words for. Then he told me a particular incident which he hoped would illustrate what he was struggling to say.

"I remember one of the times I was really frightened. There was a guy in our outfit who was probably the worst, most vicious animal I've ever seen. He'd sit down and like to talk about the tortures he had inflicted on people. I really hated that guy. Most of the time, I can empathize with cruel people, because I can usually tell, at least intellectually, what that person has gone through. I knew I had no right to hate this guy, but he really affected me.

"On this particular day, we were all in a creek bed. This guy was in charge, and he was a very avid warrior, as it were; he wanted to pursue the enemy. The majority of us were more interested in letting the pursued people escape. Actually, we were following a force much larger than ourselves, even though we didn't know it at the time.

"It was really beautiful in the creek bed, in a way only the Nam can be beautiful. It's wild and clean, and it's not polluted; can you image—you can drink the water and breathe the air? It's astounding!

"Suddenly we were ambushed by a very large force. People got split up, and we were confused. Then it was decided we were going to try to run out of it. It was terrifying, people were popping up and down; it was a riot, a tremendous turmoil, weird, and oh, God, we finally got to the top of the hill, and managed to consolidate there somehow.

"We got everyone together to figure out who was missing. When we found them, four were dead. They were lying on the ground, their heads covered, and their feet were exposed.

"Then I recognized this guy I hated. He was dead instead of me. I was alive; wow, I thought. I was *glad* he was dead, and that was a terrifying thought. It made me feel a little sick and ashamed, but in a practical sense it was good he was dead, because the amount of pain he had brought to the world greatly exceeded his value.

"The next morning I woke up early and watched the sunrise. The mountains were right in front of me, abrupt, so steep, they go right from the top straight to the bottom. They have so many beautiful things in them—waterfalls, weird, distorted shapes.

"For a while, I was depressed. I really thought about it

a lot. But gradually, almost as if I couldn't help it, a kind of exuberance built up, and finally, I just felt so good to be able to be alive, and ran up and down."

About the Author

Malcolm Boyd, long a leader in the peace movement and civil rights, was ordained an Episcopal priest in 1955. He is the author of *Are You Running With Me, Jesus?; Free to Live, Free to Die; As I Live and Breathe: Stages of an Autobiography*. He was in residence at Yale University as a Guest Fellow in 1968–1969, and has lectured on university campuses throughout the United States and Canada. A playwright and film critic, he has also given public readings of his written works, accompanied by distinguished American musicians. Boston University has established the Malcolm Boyd Collection, a permanent archive in its library for the priest-author's papers and writings.